BORDERLINE STATES IN PSYCHIATRY

SEMINARS IN PSYCHIATRY

Series Editor
Milton Greenblatt, M.D.
Chief, Psychiatry Service
Veterans Administration Hospital
Sepulveda, California, and
Professor of Psychiatry
University of California, Los Angeles

Other Books in Series:

Psychiatric Aspects of Neurologic Disease, edited by D. Frank Benson, M.D., and Dietrich Blumer, M.D. (in press)

Topics in Psychoendocrinology, edited by Edward J. Sachar, M.D. (in press)

Suicidology: Current Developments, edited by Edwin S. Shneidman, M.D. (in press)

Drugs in Combination with Other Therapies, edited by Milton Greenblatt, M.D. (in press)

Consultation-Liaison Psychiatry, edited by Robert O. Pasnau, M.D. (in press)

BORDERLINE STATES IN PSYCHIATRY

Edited by
John E. Mack, M.D.
Chief of Psychiatry
The Cambridge Hospital
and
Clinical Director
The Cambridge-Somerville Mental Health Center
and
Professor of Psychiatry
The Cambridge Hospital
Harvard Medical School, Boston

GRUNE & STRATTON
A Subsidiary of Harcourt Brace Jovanovich, Publishers
New York   San Francisco   London

Library of Congress Cataloging in Publication Data
Main entry under title:
Borderline states in psychiatry.

  (Seminars in psychiatry)
  Includes index.
  1. Pseudoneurotic schizophrenia. I. Mack, John
E., 1929–   [DNLM: 1. Mental disorders.
2. Mental disorders—Diagnosis. WM100 B728]
RC514.B59   616.8'982   75-14406
ISBN 0-8089-0878-2

Grune & Stratton, Inc.
111 Fifth Avenue
New York, New York 10033

Distributed in the United Kingdom by
Academic Press, Inc. (London) Ltd.
24/28 Oval Road, London NW1

Library of Congress Catalog Card Number 75-14406
International Standard Book Number 0-8089-0878-2
Printed in the United States of America

Contents

Foreword

The distinguished psychiatrist, C. Mac Phie Campbell, in trying to convey to students the heterogeneity of individuals lumped under the diagnosis of *schizophrenia,* used to teach that schizophrenia was less a disease than a territory. Although there lived in this territory persons of widely different temperaments, life styles, values, and customs, nevertheless, there was a sufficient degree of commonality among them so that it was possible to communicate some meaning to professionals by the use of the term.

There also exists in psychiatry a vast borderland in which live individuals even more heterogeneous than those in the territory labeled schizophrenia. Here and there in this no man's land, clinicians are beginning to discern persons who they believe are worthy of nosologic identification. The clinicians claim that these individuals possess particular character deviations, ego defects, and ways of relating to people that differentiate them from others. Further, in dealing with these individuals on an intimate, long-term basis, they respond, it is claimed, in a typical way to technical maneuvers. Thus, the identification of new groupings in this borderland is of more than academic significance.

The borderland has fascinated clinicians for years. Recently, with the renewal of concentration on character disorders and ego pathology, interest has surged markedly—matched, we are pleased to say, by vigorous intellectual efforts to establish better boundaries in this uncertain terrain. More than once in the past, workers have come together to share experiences, to identify case types, to review psychodynamics, and to try to formulate researchable hypotheses. Does the borderland, for example, lie between the psychoses and normality, between the psychoses and the neuroses, or between the neuroses and some other condition? What phenomenological, dynamic, and life-course features shall we look for to identify case types?

There seems to be a conviction among clinicians working in different settings that the same patient types can be recognized in a variety of milieux—on hospital wards, in ambulatory clinics, in prisons, and so forth—and that the characteristic "splitting" psychopathology may also be found in their families. The two-way interaction between the borderline patient and the milieu can give rise to very interesting complications in management; this should give the reader food for thought.

There are two chapters in this noteworthy volume that are particularly significant; one on the effects of drugs in borderline cases and the other on the problem of supervision of residents therapeutically involved with them.

It is difficult to conceive how Dr. John Mack, topic editor, and the contributors whom he selected could have done more to update thinking in the field or to provide a more fair-minded critique of present concepts. It is our hope, therefore, that this volume will be useful to psychiatrists challenged to cope with these borderline patients and particularly that it will stir their imagination and initiative to undertake definitive observations and research in this area.

MILTON GREENBLATT, M.D.
Editor-in-Chief
Seminars in Psychiatry

Preface

The purpose of this volume is to examine the current status of the borderline concept as a diagnostic term or entity in psychiatry. Essays have been included that reflect the use that various practitioners, approaching their clinical cases from differing perspectives and working in different settings, make of the borderline concept.

Gerald Adler looks at a large group of patients, predominantly in ambulatory settings, for whom he has found the diagnosis of borderline to be useful. Howard A. Wishnie examines the group of patients called borderline on a general hospital inpatient ward. Daniel H. Jacobs considers the applicability of the borderline diagnosis and associated phenomena to a population of prisoners. Samuel B. Guze applies the standards of differential diagnosis to the borderline diagnostic category, while Donald F. Klein examines the borderline entity from the point of view of a clinician who has found the response to psychopharmacological agents to be useful in differentiating psychiatric disorders. James F. Masterson describes the predominant psychological mechanisms in adolescents to whom he applies the borderline diagnosis. John Zinner and Edward R. Shapiro look at the psychodynamics of family life in patients diagnosed as borderline. John T. Maltsberger and Dan H. Buie examine the emotional responses and special difficulties of the physician or psychotherapist treating this troubled patient population.

My own introductory chapter is concerned with the history of the "borderline" term or concept and how it has come to have such prominence. There will not be a complete review of the large body of literature on or related to this subject; instead selected works that indicate significant trends will be described.

JOHN E. MACK, M.D.

Contributors

Gerald Adler, M.D.,
Associate Professor of Psychiatry,
New England Medical Center Hospitals,
Boston, Massachusetts.

Daniel H. Jacobs, M.D.,
Instructor in Psychiatry,
The Cambridge Hospital,
Harvard Medical School,
Cambridge, Massachusetts;
Director of Court Clinic for Third District Court,
Middlesex County, Massachusetts.

Dan H. Buie, M.D.,
Associate Professor of Psychiatry,
Tufts University School of Medicine,
Boston, Massachusetts.

Samuel B. Guze, M.D.,
Vice Chancellor for Medical Affairs,
Department of Psychiatry,
Barnes and Renard Hospitals;
Spencer T. Olin Professor of Psychiatry,
Washington University School of Medicine,
St. Louis, Missouri.

Donald F. Klein, M.D.,
Director Research and Evaluation,
Department of Psychiatry,
Long Island Jewish-Hillside Medical Center,
Glen Oaks, New York;
Professor of Psychiatry,
State University of New York,
Stony Brook;
Adjunct Professor of Psychology,
Queens College,
City University of New York,
New York, New York.

John E. Mack, M.D.,
Chief of Psychiatry,
The Cambridge Hospital;
Clinical Director,
The Cambridge-Somerville Mental Health Center;
Professor of Psychiatry,
The Cambridge Hospital,

Harvard Medical School,
Boston, Massachusetts.

John T. Maltsberger, M.D.,
Assistant Clinical Professor of Psychiatry,
Harvard Medical School,
Boston, Massachusetts.

James F. Masterson, M.D.,
Clinical Professor of Psychiatry,
Cornell University Medical College;
Head Adolescent Program,
New York Hospital (Payne Whitney Clinic),
New York, New York.

Edward R. Shapiro, M.D.,
Instructor in Psychiatry,
Harvard Medical School,
Boston, Massachusetts;
Assistant Psychiatrist,
Director Adolescent and Family Treatment and Study
    Center,
McLean Hospital,
Belmont, Massachusetts.

John Zinner, M.D.,
Clinical Associate Professor,
Department of Psychiatry and Behavioral Sciences,
George Washington University Medical Center,
Washington, D.C.

Howard A. Wishnie, M.D.,
Instructor in Psychiatry,
Harvard Medical School;
Director, Inpatient Psychiatry Service,
The Cambridge Hospital,
Cambridge, Massachusetts.

BORDERLINE STATES IN PSYCHIATRY

John E. Mack

1

Borderline States:
An Historical Perspective

From the time that they were first introduced into the psychiatric and psychoanalytic literature, terms such as borderline state and borderline psychosis have been met with a mixed reception. Some writers found these terms to be either imprecise or misleading[41,54,63,106] while others found them to be more useful.[5,20,58,72,93] In recent years the term *borderline* has attained a popularity that its rather inauspicious beginnings would not have led one to anticipate. Leston L. Havens wrote recently that until a few years ago "the great thing was to mourn. Now the magic word is 'borderline.'"[49]

The value of diagnostic terms becomes established as they demonstrate their power to bring about clearer and more precise clinical description and a deepening of dynamic understanding. In the long run these tests will undoubtedly be applied to the term borderline. For the time being it is obvious that the borderline concept has taken hold. The degree of interest that has been aroused in borderline states was evident when a panel of papers delivered at the May 1974 meeting of the American Psychiatric Association drew a huge overflow crowd. Of 117 consecutive admissions to a psychiatric inpatient service from February to June 1974, 15 received the label "borderline" while only 7 received any other diagnosis in the broad category of character and behavior disorders.[84] It is hardly possible to attend a case conference in which the expression is not either applied to the patient under consideration or used to compare him or her with other patients.

BORDERLINES AND BORDERLANDS IN THE HISTORY
OF PSYCHIATRY

The borderline concept as it is currently used resembles a large reservoir into which have flowed many streams from our psychiatric and psychoanalytic past. The attempt to delineate a recognizable "borderline" entity with clearly defined descriptive features derives from adherence to the nosology of Kraepelinian psychiatry. At the same time the influence of psychoanalytic concepts and discoveries, especially in the areas of character formation and character pathology, had led to efforts to establish the developmental and structural basis of the disorder, or disorders, to which the borderline label is applied.

The psychiatry of the eighteenth and much of the nineteenth centuries is the psychiatry of the asylum and of unreason, in which "the man of reason delegates the physician to madness" and the physician as the man of reason separates himself from the men he would call mad.[31] Until the past century medical psychology or psychiatry concerned itself chiefly with the insane, i.e., with individuals incarcerated or kept in asylums (those now called "inpatients") because of their defects of reason. Not until Philippe Pinel recognized that there were some madmen who retained their powers or reasoning—*mania sans délire*[81]— did it become possible for psychiatrists to devote their attention to the vast group of troubled individuals who retain their appreciation of reality but manifest their disturbances in disordered behavior and emotional anguish.

It remained for James Cowles Prichard in England in the first half of the nineteenth century to recognize that in addition to the traditional forms of "unreasoning" insanity there is "likewise a form of mental derangement in which the intellectual faculties appear to have sustained little or no injury, while the disorder is manifested principally alone, in the state of the feelings, temper or habits."[82] Such individuals, Prichard wrote, were also impaired in their power of "self-government." He called this disorder "moral insanity" and defined it as "madness consisting in a morbid perversion of the natural feelings, affections, inclinations, temper, habits, moral disposition, and natural impulses, without any remarkable disorder or defect of the intellect or knowing and reasoning faculties, and particularly without any insane illusion or hallucination."[82] Prichard included, in his case examples of moral insanity, many patients whom we would now classify in the psychoneurotic, addictive, personality disorder, or even manic-depressive categories. The concept of moral insanity enabled European and American psychiatrists to consider a vast group of patients and disorders that they had not previously considered as falling within their purview.

In Prichard's concept the moral faculties seem to have included the will and temperament in addition to the ethical aspects of the mind, and his "moral insanity" was thus a broadly inclusive entity. However, because of certain influences affecting nineteenth-century European psychiatry, especially the spread of the concept of degeneration, a far more restricted use of "moral" developed, and moral insanity became more narrowly and pejoratively defined. As late as 1923, Eugen Bleuler was still using such terms as moral idiots and moral oligophrenics, together with moral insanity, to designate the "enemies of society"—those with "constitutional ethical aberrations."[10] According to the religious and moralistic theory of degeneration, of which insanity was the outstanding example, "the first generation of a degenerate family might be merely nervous, the second would tend to be neurotic, the third psychotic, while the fourth consisted of idiots and died out."[4] Prichard's moral insanity lent itself conveniently to the development of a diagnostic grouping that he did not seem to have in mind—the psychopathic personality. Moral insanity was largely replaced toward the end of the nineteenth century by "psychopathic inferiority," a term invented by J. L. Koch to designate a group of criminals and other defective individuals who committed various types of antisocial acts as a result of some sort of constitutional inferiority.[70]

At the turn of the twentieth century, the term *constitutional psychopathic inferiority* gained great popularity in both Europe and America. Emil Kraepelin added to the later editions of his textbook, beginning about 1905, many pages of new material on constitutional psychopathic states and psychopathic personalities; some of those so labeled were said to bear the marks or stigmata of Cesare Lombroso's born criminal.[24,69] Bleuler soon followed suit.[10] Kraepelin was aware that he was entering a vast and little charted area (coinciding roughly with our character and borderline groups) whose various margins were poorly defined. "These various forms of the insanity of degeneration are hard to group," he wrote, "because there are so many combinations and border-line states."[24] Such states in Kraepelin's view occupied the borderline between insanity and the various eccentricities of individuals who were normal or merely odd. "Those psychopathic conditions which develop on a morbid constitutional basis include," he wrote, "an extensive borderland between pronounced morbid states and mere personality eccentricities which are wont to be regarded as normal."[24] Another German psychiatrist, C. Pelman, published a book in 1909 on the "borderland" states of mind, among which he included criminals, alcoholics, suicidal patients, perversions, and "social disorders."[80] Pelman likened reason and insanity to two circles in which the area of overlap was the borderland. These borderline cases were, according to Pelman, inferior individuals who were examples of degeneration. He thought that the universities were seeing more such cases!

Although Kraepelin had included in his psychopathic groups various psychoneurotic and unstable individuals, between 1910 and 1930 the term psychopath came increasingly to be restricted to individuals exhibiting antisocial tendencies of various sorts.* The broad area of other personality disorders and borderlands were neglected once again, except in restricted instances. In 1930 G. E. Partridge in the United States suggested that the diagnosis of psychopathic personality be done away with because it was too inclusive. He introduced the term *sociopathic* to distinguish the group of personality disorders with specific antisocial tendencies from the rest of the group.[79] This distinction, Partridge felt, would encourage attention to other personality deviations that were not antisocial.

DEVELOPMENTS IN PSYCHOANALYSIS: CHARACTER AND CHARACTER PATHOLOGY

Terms from general psychiatry, such as schizoid and cyclothymic personality, were popular for describing certain personality types thought to resemble or be related to the classic functional psychoses. At about the same time, from Freudian psychoanalysis, character types related to libidinal phases of development (oral, anal, and so on) began to be recognized as were the extraverted and introverted types of Carl Jung.

During the same period that the borderlands of the psychopathies were being described in European and American psychiatry, psychoanalysis was developing a body of data and an approach to patients that would also soon contribute to the understanding of a number of borderland areas of psychiatry. Sigmund Freud, together with most of his European colleagues, worked largely with patients seen in an office practice. Freud himself, of course, began his practice as a neurologist. He valued the opportunity to learn about psychotic cases from Jung and others among his coworkers who had access to psychiatric cases in hospitals and sanatoria. But most of the early psychoanalytic re-

---

*This was probably because these forms of behavior more frequently brought the patient and the psychiatrist together in the mental hospital and the courtroom.

searches were concerned with less severe disorders. Although the psychoanalytic discoveries regarding the formation and psychopathology of character were made in the course of studying allegedly psychoneurotic cases, these data and concepts were later to have particular value for the understanding of more severe disturbances.

Initially Freud and his coworkers were no more interested in the study of character or personality in its own right than were the hospital psychiatrists. Not until relatively recently have character and personality been considered legitimate objects of medical investigation. Rather, the early psychoanalysts were primarily interested in uncovering the unconscious drives, especially childhood sexual impulses, which, when too vigorously banished from conscious awareness, were thought to bring about neurotic suffering. They discovered, almost by accident it seemed, that certain erotic inclinations seemed regularly to be associated with particular character traits. Beginning with Freud's paper, "Character and Anal Erotism" in 1908, Freud, Karl Abraham, Ernest Jones, and others tried to document over two decades the development of the libidinal stages and the particular erotic drive components that were associated with the formation of such character traits as generosity, stinginess, and ambition.[1-3,33,55] Through his familiarity with a limited number of psychotic cases, some of which were brought to his attention by Jung, Freud also began to appreciate the role of narcissism in the more severe mental disturbances and of the narcissistic defenses of projection, denial and distortion, through which the individual seeks to preserve his self-regard and the integrity of his personality at the expense of reality and relationships with others.[34]

Between 1914 and 1932 Freud developed out of his clinical experience the theoretical concepts that have been most relevant in psychoanalysis for the understanding of character formation and most useful for clarifying the psychological mechanisms operative in the psychoses and in severe character disorders. During this period Freud evolved his structural theory of personality, described the ego and its defenses, clarified the mechanisms of identification, and demonstrated the central role of conflict related to anxiety and unconscious guilt in the formation of pathological structures and in the causation of maladaptive personality responses. The clinical studies of early child development and the observations of the early conflict situations of small children by Anna Freud, Melanie Klein, and other child analysts were also to prove of value in the understanding of adult character formation and for later psychopathology.[32,62]

The Austrian psychiatrist Wilhelm Reich and the Hungarian Franz Alexander deserve credit for the first systematic application of Freudian ego psychological concepts to the study of pathological character types. Reich, crediting Freud's 1923 monograph, *The Ego and the Id,* with laying "the groundwork for a psychoanalytically based theory of character" proceeded over the decade following its publication to provide classical psychoanalytic characterizations of the clinical features of the impulsive, compulsive, hysterical, masochistic, and other character types.[85] Reich's attention, like Freud's, was drawn to the importance of pathological character traits as a secondary result of his treatment efforts. He found that the various discrete character formations operated as resistances or as a defensive armor and interfered with the analyst's approach to warded-off memories and disturbing instinctual demands. This "character armor," Reich showed, could not be ignored or bypassed in the treatment process. Rather, it had to be confronted, interpreted, and even "smashed." As a result of his struggles with the various forms of character resistance, Reich developed an important body of understanding of groups of patients that had not hitherto been familiar to analysts and psychiatrists.

Reich's long classic paper on the Impulsive Character (*Der Triebhafte Charakter*) appeared first in German in 1925. It was not translated into English until 1970 and then only in the *Journal of Orgonomy,* edited by followers of Reich who remained with him during his later career.* In his 1925 paper Reich described the ambivalence, the dominance of pregenital hostile impulses, the ego and superego defects, the immaturity of defensive organization, and the primitive narcissism of impulsive personalities. He recognized explicitly that in impulsive and other character disorders he was dealing with a type of borderline case and frequently used that term. "It is all the same," Reich wrote, "if we say the neurotic character, the impulsive character, and the psychopath constitute borderline cases between psychosis and health," and, "we lay no particular stress on the viewpoint we take here that the impulsive character is a borderline case between symptom neurosis and psychosis on the basis of his particular defense mechanism."[86]

Franz Alexander in 1927 described in the terms of psychoanalytic theories of neurotic conflict formation a large group of patients, resembling Reich's impulsive characters in a number of ways, who manifested their psychopathology not in discrete symptom formation but in "an irrational style of life dominated by unconscious motives."[7] He called this type of person "the neurotic character" and described a number of individuals, some of whom resemble the borderlines of our

---

*While this manuscript was being prepared, Reich's work has become available in English in a paperback volume.[86]

contemporary literature—individuals "driven by demonic compulsion." In fact, in the first psychoanalytic paper specifically devoted to borderline cases as such, A. Stern wrote in 1938 that the "neurotic character ... makes up a very large proportion of this borderline group."[93] Alexander called these individuals, who direct their energies toward the outside world, "alloplastic" and wrote that "the case history of a neurotic character reads like a novel with plenty of action."[7] He distinguished neurotic characters from the symptom neurotic, the psychotic, the patient with a perversion, and the true criminal, believing that the latter did not suffer from conflict.

PSYCHOANALYSIS IN THE UNITED STATES AND ITS APPLICATION TO THE BORDERLANDS OF PSYCHIATRY

Nowhere in the world did psychoanalytic concepts find the acceptance in medicine and psychiatry that they did in the United States. Between 1905 and 1914 Adolf Meyer, Abraham Brill, James Jackson Putnam, G. Stanley Hall, William Alanson White, and others introduced Freudian concepts into psychiatric hospital treatment and private practice. From 1914 onward there was a steady development of psychoanalytic practice and education, and psychoanalytic societies were formed in several cities.*

It is most likely the success of this relationship—between psychoanalytic thinking and psychiatric practice—that accounts for the fact that concern with borderlines and borderline states has been primarily an American preoccupation. Papers on this subject published outside of the United States are actually quite rare. In Europe, where psychoanalytic thinking has had less impact on general psychiatric practice, the borderlands continue to be filled with a great variety of pathological character types and a borderline state as such is not recognized.**

The application of psychoanalytic theoretical concepts and modified treatment approaches to hospitalized patients has also led to an in-

*John C. Burnham, in his *Psychoanalysis and American Medicine, 1894-1918: Medicine, Science and Culture,* has analyzed the factors in American culture and science which account for the unexpectedly successful reception which psychoanalysis had in this country.[13]

**Even the most recent American Psychiatric Association *Diagnostic and Statistical Manual* published in 1968 (DSM-II) recognizes more than 35 character or personality disturbances but has no borderline classifications.

creased attention to borderland and borderline cases in the United States. "Very largely because psycho-analysis in America has been unswervingly sponsored by a group of well-trained psychiatrists," C. P. Oberndorf wrote in 1930, "the tendency to infuse psycho-analytic concepts into borderline cases has been more general here than abroad."[78] As early as 1919 Pierce Clark wrote about "borderland neuroses and psychoses," among which he included severe neurotics, certain depressives, and six or seven mild cases of dementia praecox.[20] Two years later T. V. Moore described a conglomeration of cases, including depressions, anxiety states, and various character problems that he called "borderline mental states . . . too simple to be termed major psychoses or even to be classed with the vague psychoneuroses."[77] By the end of the 1930s it was recognized by some American psychiatrists and psychoanalysts that they were seeing patients both in hospitals and in private practice "far removed from the textbook descriptions" of psychotic and psychoneurotic cases and "progressing a step beyond the realm of simple neuroses, between the severer neuroses and the milder psychoses."[78] In Europe this realm continued to be lumped together largely as psychopathic reactions or psychopathies.*

Although Stern and other psychoanalysts recognized the existence of large groups of patients who were on the one hand not overtly psychotic but who at the same time manifested an infantile defensive organization, low self-esteem, and a tendency to act out psychic conflict, these analysts rarely used the term borderline and in many instances actively resisted it. Instead, analytically oriented psychiatrists during the 1930s concentrated on the understanding of the psychic conflicts underlying specific pathological character types or problems. Ives Hendrick, for example, described the particular relationship among certain pregenital anxieties, early childhood conflicts related to aggression, and familiar character disturbances, such as schizoid, passive-dependent, and paranoid personalities.[51] Helene Deutsch described a particular character disturbance that she called the "as-if" personality.[22] Patients so designated had disturbed relationships with others and adult attachments that were superficial and imitative, much like a small child's. These patients, primarily women in Deutsch's examples, had not experienced healthy emotional contact with their mothers. This resulted in a failure of internalization, identification, and normal ego and superego formation.

Other analysts during this period applied concepts of early personality

---

*See, for example, the 1924 American translation of Bleuler's *Textbook of Psychiatry.*[10]

development to the study of perversions,[42] delinquency,[6] criminality,[43] and instinct-ridden and other character disorders.[30] Reich in his 1925 paper had stressed that people with severe character disorders, especially impulsive characters, were borderline cases. He believed that "the question of borderline cases warrants considerable discussion."[86] Borderline cases for Reich and the other early students of character pathology simply displayed disorders of character or personality for whom the prevailing neurotic and psychotic diagnoses were not applicable. A specific borderline diagnosis seems not to have been needed. Edward Glover, for example, in his 1932 paper on the classification of mental disorders acknowledged that he had "represented the addictions as true 'borderline' states in the sense that they have one foot in the psychoses and the other in the neuroses," but he then objected to the terms "borderline" and "pre"-psychotic.[41] "If a psychotic mechanism is present at all," Glover insisted, "it should be given a definite label." Freud himself in his preface to August Aichhorn's study of delinquent youths wrote of the value of applying psychoanalytic knowledge to the study of "borderline and mixed cases," but he never specifically applied the term borderline to a particular group of patients. Perhaps he recognized that the boundaries that separate one type of disorder from another, and the healthy from the clinically disordered, are too vague and variable to permit their discrete delineation.

Gregory Zilboorg in 1941 took a view similar to Glover's. He identified a group of patients who shared in common the failure to integrate reality into their affective lives.[106] He included in this group psychopathic personalities, "poor" personalities, transvestites, fetishists, and other sexual perverts, and murderers as well as mild-mannered quiet, unobtrusive, and ineffective people. These are people, Zilboorg observed, who are suffused with hatred and inner rage. However, Zilboorg rejected "the euphemistic labels of borderline cases, incipient schizophrenias, schizoid personalities, mixed manic-depressive psychoses, schizoid manics, or psychopathic personalities." He preferred to lump them all together with the term "ambulatory schizophrenias," believing that the diagnosis of schizophrenia should not be reserved for the more severe or untreatable cases.

In 1949 Paul H. Hoch and Phillip Polatin applied the term "pseudoneurotic schizophrenia" to a group of patients whom they distinguished from psychoneurotics and obvious schizophrenics.[54] These patients appeared superficially to resemble neurotics, but their symptoms were more diverse (panneurosis) and their anxiety more pervasive and profound (pananxiety). Behind the neurotic facade, the authors observed, these patients demonstrated schizophrenic-like disturbances of thought and affect and thus, in their opinion, were schizophrenics in a kind of psychoneurotic disguise. Although the concept of pseudoneurotic schizophrenia continued to be pursued by Hoch and his associates, it has found only a limited following.[23,52,53]

Melitta Schmideberg, with her characteristic intuition and somewhat impressionistic clinical approach, recognized a large group of cases whom she labeled borderline. They were individuals with difficulty adapting to the real world and to whom something was always happening.[90] Schmideberg wrote that she had treated 100 such cases, but she, like Zilboorg, lumped together in her description psychopathic personalities, criminals, alcoholics, and paranoids as well as various other acting-out and suicidal individuals.

THE EMERGENCE OF A BORDERLINE GROUPING

By 1950 most psychiatrists seem to have been convinced (there were exceptions) that they were seeing a large group of patients who were not strictly speaking schizophrenic, according to Bleuler's criteria, and yet were more severely disturbed than the patients they were accustomed to calling psychoneurotic.[26,94,103] V. W. Eisenstein, for example, reported in 1951 that 30 percent of 250 consecutive cases seen at two outpatient clinics in the New York City area were "such borderline reaction types."[26] Casework agencies in Boston reported similar experiences.[56,99] Although the patients being diagnosed borderline demonstrated serious character disturbances and a kind of "emotional infantilism,"[96] these traits were varied and poorly described, and the group as a whole did not fit itself exclusively into one disorder of character or another.

Some clarity was brought to the situation by Robert P. Knight with his publication in 1953 of two papers on the diagnosis, psychodynamics, and treatment of borderline patients.[63,64] He stated explicitly that he had no wish to defend the diagnosis of borderline states but sought rather to bring together the phenomena that seemed generally to be associated with the diagnosis of borderline in the literature. He described a variety of ego defenses and disturbances of object relationships.[63] Knight recommended that in making a diagnosis a complete inventory of ego functioning be undertaken in order to assess the balance between the ego's strengths, on the one hand, and the disruptive environmental and instinctual forces, on the other. He cautioned against the exclusive and uncritical acceptance of assumptions from both traditional psychiatry and psychoanalysis: such as that "break with reality" must be total; that neurosis and psychosis are mutually exclusive in a given case; or that the defense mechanisms employed by the ego can be explicitly correlated with particular fixations and points of regression in the development of the libido. These warnings often have not been followed in the extensive literature on borderlines published in the two decades since Knight published his papers. Knight also described the modifications of the treatment setting, the need for a reality-oriented approach with firm limit setting, and other modifications of psychoanalytic therapeutic technique necessary for working with patients designated as borderlines.

Following the publication of Knight's papers, the American Psychoanalytic Association gave official recognition to the borderline problem by holding two all-day panels in May 1954 and December 1955 on "The Borderline Case".[83,87] Many of the researchers mentioned in the preceding pages were brought together. In the first meeting Elizabeth R. Zetzel objected to the borderline diagnosis on the grounds that there are no sharp borders to be delineated and that such a term tended to remove the necessity of making further effort to achieve diagnostic refinement. Zilboorg, who was present at the first panel meeting, also remained severely critical of the borderline concept. "There is a psychiatric area of theoretical penumbra, called by some 'borderline,' " he wrote in 1956, "in which there reigns considerable chaos or confusion with regard to clinical criteria and diagnostic differentiation. In this area the clinical psychiatrist who adheres to descriptive nosology feels free to use newer concepts and terminology and yet fails to clarify the confusion of the borderland; in the same area the psychoanalyst feels free to use some of the traditional nosological criteria, and yet fails to clarify the chaos of the penumbra."[106] Zilboorg clung to his "ambulatory schizophrenias" for these patients in the "borderland"—a concept that did little to reduce the chaos or illuminate the penumbra.

At the second panel of the American Psychoanalytic Association on "The Borderline Case" Melitta Schmideberg presented a paper entitled "Principles of Directive Analytic Therapy for Borderline Patients," which she elaborated in a long essay that appeared in 1959 in the *American Handbook of Psychiatry*.[91] Schmideberg took a step toward relating the psychopathology of the borderline states to the character disorders. The borderline patients, she wrote, were a group, stabile in their instability, whose disturbed ego and social functioning affected every area of their lives. These patients had features in common with—borders with—normal and neurotic individuals, psychopaths, and psychotic patients but in her opinion (in comparison with her earlier view) did not fit into any of these categories.

Much of the remainder of the second panel seems to have been taken up with expressions of concern about the harm that the modifications of treatment technique necessary in treating "borderline" cases (whoever they were) might do to psychoanalysis. At the meeting Jan Frank[87] introduced a genetic approach to the understanding of the ego development of borderline patients that was later to be developed by Arnold H. Modell. Frank suggested that the personalities of these patients might be understood through the application of Donald W. Winnicott's concept of "the transitional object phase" of development. In choosing to look at the borderline cases as individuals with "a different ego which is not necessarily defective in the sense of something being lacking," Frank seems to have been inviting those present to depart from thinking of their patients solely from the standpoint of the polarity of health and pathology. He spoke of explorers, rebels, writers, scientists, and other gifted or creative individuals capable of great achievement under appropriate circumstances whose egos might seem so different to a clinical observer as to evoke improperly the diagnosis of borderline or be given some other pathological label.

The differentiating of a group of adult borderline patients by Knight, Schmideberg, and other psychoanalysts in the 1950s stimulated the child analysts to reexamine their caseloads from this point of view. Not much more than ten years earlier Leo Kanner had described clearly for the first time a group of psychotic or "autistic" children. Beginning with a paper by Rudolph Ekstein and J. Wallerstein in 1954, child analysts over the next few years became aware that they, like their coworkers in the adult field, were seeing a number of children who, on the one hand, were distinguishable from frankly psychotic children and adolescents but who, on the other hand, were more severely disturbed than their psychoneurotic patients.[27,40] These "borderline" children demonstrated serious disturbances of ego development; in contrast to psychotic children, they showed more fluctuation in their functional capacities and demonstrated more areas of ego strength. Clinically the borderline children were characterized by their proneness to anxieties of an overwhelming intensity (panic reactions); they were vulnerable to ego regression and fragmentation when confronted with conventional stresses. To a greater extent than neurotic or normal children, the borderline cases showed a tendency toward grandiose and magical thinking and an inclination to treat their fantasy productions as real. In contrast to the psychotic children, reality testing was maintained in the borderline cases or reality was recoverable when the stresses producing the regression and decompensation were no longer operative, i.e., the brief episodes of frank psychosis from which they suffered at times were reversible. The borderline cases demonstrated markedly disturbed relationships with others, and a disturbed early relationship with the mother was postulated. However, the precise nature of this early disturbance was not determined.

Of 100 cases that Robert L. Arnstein saw in 1958 at a college health clinic, he distinguished 20 young men whom he called borderline.[9] He then divided these 20 into four groups. Five suffered from continuing serious social disability; six had a distinct but short-lived psychotic crisis; three had classic but circumscribed psychotic symptoms; while the fourth group consisted of withdrawn or schizoid individuals. Arnstein found that he was able to help these young men with psychotherapy; however, he was least successful with the withdrawn group. His paper on his work with these college men is of value because within the group designated borderline it attempts to differentiate among the patients, to take into account the life circumstances and the role of stresses related to a particular period of life, and, finally, to distinguish between fixed characterological or relatively permanent psychopathological structures and more transient psychological reactions.

DEVELOPMENTS SINCE 1960

The focus in discussions of borderline states has shifted since 1960 from attention to the determination and exploration of their phenomenology to a detailed examination of the underlying character organization, infantile fixations, qualities of object relationships, and treatment of patients to whom the borderline diagnosis is applied. It appears as if once a consensus could be assumed as to the *existence* of a complex and difficult group of patients designated as borderline, the further clarification of observable clinical phenomena, and the differentiating of patients within this broad category, might be bypassed in favor of a search for underlying psychological mechanisms and the development of treatment approaches. In 1967 E. Rolde reviewed from a sociocultural perspective the status of the concept of "character disorders," including the literature on borderline states.[88] He concluded that definitions of borderline remained hazy and that the clinical diagnosis was often made on the basis of impressions rather than according to generally accepted criteria. John Frosch remarked in a paper published in 1970, "It is remarkable that in an area where there exists so much confusion in nosology, one finds agreement on so many aspects of the therapeutic approach."[39]

In 1963 Modell introduced the transference in the psychoanalytic or the psychotherapy setting as an instrument for diagnostic differentiation.[74] He recognized that many types of personality might be diagnosed as borderline and that the transference relationship with the therapist could be a "useful operational method" of diagnosing these patients. Drawing upon the developmental concepts of Donald W. Winnicott, a child therapist and analyst, Modell likened the transference relationships that borderline patients establish with their analysts or therapists to the attachment to a "transitional object," such as a teddy bear or blanket, that small children form as they attempt to become more autonomous beings, separate from their mothers. Consequently borderline patients bring their conflicts with the environment directly into the transference relationship. Modell postulated that because of a disordered early relationship with the mother the borderline patient has become arrested developmentally at this transitional-object stage of character formation and human relationships. Such a patient seeks in the therapist an omnipotent magical protector. He confuses himself with the therapist and at the same time fears intensely human closeness, believing that his own loving feelings possess destructive power. According to Modell, ego functioning is more stable in the borderline disorder than in the schizophrenic; ties to others are maintained, and the disorder involves the personality less totally.

In papers published in 1963 and 1965 S. Kut Rosenfeld and M. P. Sprince applied the emerging theories of early object relationships to the understanding of a group of children thought to be borderline.[66,67] They suggested that the ego disturbances observed in these children were due to a failure of early internalization in the relationship with the mothering person. These children retained, according to the authors, an "as-if" quality in their later relationships—somewhere between identification and object attachment—that were at all times precarious and associated with fear of annihilation and disintegration. The authors make the interesting observation that the borderline child, in contrast to the psychotic child, establishes a higher level of ego functioning in some areas than his capacity for object relations would lead one to expect.*

Using schizophrenic psychoses as his frame of reference, Frosch distinguished from "among the so-called borderline conditions" a subgroup that he called "the psychotic character."[38,39] The psychotic character is "the more crystalized borderline personality" and has in common with the "true" psychotic personality seriously disturbed object relationships, primitive ego defenses that permit the breakthrough into consciousness of id material, and severely impaired adaptive capacities

---

*See also C. Malone[72] in regard to precocious ego functioning in children with troubled human relationships.

and relationships to reality. The person with a psychotic character is however, to be distinguished from the psychotic by his ability to preserve the capacity for reality testing and by his greater capacity for object relationships at a "need-satisfying" level in contrast to the supposed near objectlessness of some psychotics. Frosch identified altered and regressive ego states that occur in the psychotic character, including significant perceptual distortions; these are more readily reversible than in frankly psychotic cases.

Since the mid-1960s there has been an increasing tendency to consider the borderline states among, or even synonymous with, the severe character disorders and to study the personality organization of borderline patients in their own right rather than in reference to psychotic illnesses. Clinicians working with these patients have sought to understand their conflicts and difficulties in ego functioning in terms of early developmental fixations. Louis Chase and his colleague William Hire have written several papers based on their extensive experience with borderline patients.[15,16,17] According to Chase and Hire, the manifest clinical picture may be quite variable. These patients "may enter treatment following suicidal attempts, marked regression, severe depression, confusional states, depersonalization, and loss of reality, on the one extreme, to less dramatic and less acute manifestations on the other, such as long-standing inability to form satisfying object relationships, psychosomatic reactions to stress, or concerns about episodic or impulsive acting out."[16] Borderline patients may show a facade of maturity and be endowed with high intellectual ability and great creative gifts, but in each instance there is a marked oral fixation and accompanying ambivalence in object relations with a basic distrust of others. In addition, borderline patients live with a precarious psychic equilibrium because of a deficient development of reality sense and sense of self. The critical task of treatment, according to Chase and Hire, is the resolution of the negative diadic transference and the establishment of a trusting relationship with the analyst or therapist.

Although not on the topic of borderline states, two papers published in 1966 by Helen H. Tartakoff and Heinz Kohut have had a bearing on the direction of work in this area.[65,97] Tartakoff in her paper, "The Normal Personality in Our Culture and the Nobel Prize Complex," described certain normal and talented persons who are preoccupied with acclaim from society and who find in society's response to their achievements reinforcement for certain omnipotent and grandiose character elements. Although these individuals may suffer from a kind of hollowness in their object relationships and are quite narcissistic individuals, they are by no means borderline cases. Tartakoff noted in the literature a growing blurring of narcissistic personality types and border-line cases. "The diagnostic category of 'narcissistic character,' " she wrote, "especially when further qualified by the term 'disorder,' continues to refer to pathology of a borderline psychotic type. This diagnostic confusion runs throughout the literature."[97]

Kohut in his paper, "Forms and Transformation of Narcissism," argued for the consideration of narcissism as a fundamental part of human psychology. Activities such as creativity, empathy, and humor represent healthy transformations of narcissism in everyday life. Narcissism in adult life is not necessarily pathological; as a matter of fact, it is employed for the achievement of mankind's highest ideals. According to Kohut, the psychological constellations related to narcissism should be studied independently and further effort should be made to understand their various forms.

One result of the studies such as those of Kohut and Tartakoff on narcissism has been the differentiation of relatively more mature and better integrated narcissistic character types. Thus the terms "borderline" or "psychotic character" are now reserved for a more severely disturbed group.[59,65,76]

Roy R. Grinker, Beatrice Werble, and Robert C. Drye published in 1968 the first systematic study of patients diagnosed as borderline cases.[44]* The authors included in the study 51 "definitely not-schizophrenic" young adults of both sexes admitted to a psychiatric in-patient service because of suicidal ideas or attempts, impulsive behavior, phobias, compulsions, alcohol or drug abuse, somatization, or temporary confusional states. They attempted to apply psychoanalytic concepts of ego functions, such as perception, language, affects and defenses, and synthetic capabilities, to observable behavior on the hospital ward recorded by the professional staff. Using a cluster technique to rate 93 behavioral measures, Grinker and his colleagues characterized four groups of patients: (1) a most severely disturbed group bordering on the psychotic; (2) a "core borderline" group displaying chaotic interpersonal relations, acting-out behavior, and much loneliness; (3) a complaint group lacking in identity, which they likened to the "as-if" personality; and (4) a less severely disturbed group bordering on the neurotic end of the spectrum. The authors were able to obtain follow-up interviews with the majority of their patients over a one- to three-and-a-half-year period. They found that only two patients (from the first group above) had become schizophrenic. The authors concluded from their

*See Chapter 6, "Psychopharmacology and the Borderline Patient," by Donald F. Klein for a detailed review of the study by Grinker, Werble, and Drye.

study that the research had confirmed the operational usefulness of behavioral observations to test psychoanalytic theoretical concepts and suggested that their study supported the claims in the professional literature that the borderline is a specific syndrome with considerable internal consistency and stability. However, the group of patients included as borderline in this study seem to show such an extensive array of clinical characteristics that it is difficult to imagine what findings could possibly have led the authors to a different conclusion.

Grinker and his associates raise the interesting question of whether the borderline syndrome is becoming more prevalent because of certain characteristics of our culture, such as the disruptions of urban life, the increase in "existential anxiety," and the various changes in family and social structure. Some support for this position may be found in a report by Norman Lazar of patients applying for treatment to the Columbia University Psychoanalytic Clinic.[68] Lazar found a greater number of patients evincing "a defective sense of identity" and more severe problems in the mastery of aggressive drives. He noted a relative increase over a twelve-year period of patients diagnosed as having character disorders as opposed to those diagnosed as being psychoneurotic. The study is complicated by the fact that in the period between 1964 and 1971 there was a nearly fivefold decrease in the total number of individuals applying to the clinic (raising an interesting social question in its own right), which suggests the possibility of a significant bias in the sample. It is not clear whether shifts in diagnostic categories reflect real changes in the patient population or, rather, an increased attention by professionals to phenomena hitherto less stressed or to diagnostic categories not previously used or less often considered. Nevertheless, Grinker and his colleagues are correct in suggesting the need for more attention to the sociocultural dimensions of diagnosis, especially in the borderline or character-behavior disorder category where the diagnosis depends so much on the patients' functioning in relation to the social environment. The authors also point out that although much attention in studies of borderline patients had been paid to the mother-child relationship, at the time of their study virtually no examination of their families had been made.*

The work of Otto F. Kernberg on borderlines and other patients suffering from various types of character pathology has had a great influence in this field.[57,58,59,60,61] In a series of papers, beginning in 1966, Kernberg has undertaken the ambitious task of reexamining the whole

---

*For a discussion of borderline patients and their families see Chapter 8, "Splitting in Families of Borderline Adolescents" by John Zinner and Edward R. Shapiro.

area of character disorders from the standpoint of the structural derivatives in the personality that result from the internalizing processes of
early object relations. He has acknowledged in this work his debt to the
British object-relations school of Melanie Klein, W. Ronald D. Fairbairn, and Donald W. Winnicott as well as to the structural theories of
Edith Jacobson and others in this country. Basing his inferences upon
clinical findings in the transference relationship, Kernberg has related
immature defensive operations—such as splitting, primitive idealization,
projective identification, denial, omnipotence, and devaluation—to
hypothesized infantile incorporation of various aspects of the primary
care-giving objects. Kernberg believes that the borderlines—whom he
prefers to call individuals with "borderline personality organization"—
are a nonneurotic and nonpsychotic group with typical symptomatic
constellations and defensive operations. However, he includes in his
description of patients with borderline personality organization individuals with polysymptomatic neuroses, including paranoid and hypo-
chondriachal trends, polymorphous perverse sexual disorders, schizoid
and cyclothymic personalities, impulse disorders, alcohol and drug addictions, and certain depressive and sadomasochistic characters.[59]

Kernberg emphasizes "splitting" as a fundamental defense
mechanism. He regards it as characteristic of patients with borderline
personality organization. In Kernberg's usage, splitting refers to the need
to keep separate introjections and identifications of opposite quality. In
order to preserve a "good" self-image and good object image in the
presence of a dangerous "bad" self-image and bad object image, the borderline patient keeps them separated or split. According to Kernberg,
this inability to synthesize contradictory self- and object images has numerous pathological consequences. In order to maintain this separation,
the individual must resort to various other primitive defensive operations
that also compromise his human relationships and functioning in the outside world.

Kernberg has postulated a hierarchy of levels of organization of
character pathology ranging from higher through intermediate to lower
levels, depending on the majority of ego and superego functions and the
quality of object relations.[59] He places the better integrated hysterical
and other psychoneurotic characters in the higher group; then puts the
oral, passive-aggressive, better functioning infantile patients and many
narcissistic personalities in the intermediate category; and reserves the
lower level for still more infantile individuals, sexual deviants, alcoholics,
addicts, antisocial personalities, psychotic characters, and individuals
with borderline personality organization. Kernberg has taken considerable pains to distinguish between patients with borderline per-

sonality organization and those with narcissistic personalities.[60,61] In both types of patients there is, according to Kernberg, a predominance of splitting or primitive dissociative mechanisms. In the narcissistic personality structure, however, there is a relatively well-integrated, though pathological, "grandiose self." This self is the result of the condensation of the real self, the ideal self, and the ideal object. It serves to stabilize the ego and protect the self-esteem of these individuals. Modell has also distinguished the borderline from the narcissistic personality, basing his distinction on the greater achievement of autonomy from the mother in the latter and a postulated more severe infantile traumatic experience in the former. The borderline remains attached to the primary object, according to Modell, while the person with a narcissistic personality attempts to become a better mother to himself.[76]

Kernberg's views, which are well argued and based on extensive clinical work, are in many ways persuasive. His postulates are, however, difficult to test, and it would be hard to find evidence that might refute some of them since they are based on intimate clinical contacts coupled with extrapolations to hypothesized infantile psychological processes, which are often preverbal and therefore not easily observed.

The concepts of early childhood development of Margaret Mahler have also been influential in recent work related to borderline patients. E.C.M. Frijling-Schreuder views the ego disturbances in the borderline states of childhood as brought about by developmental arrest in the separation-individuation phase.[37] James F. Masterson in a study of borderline adolescents has found Mahler's concepts of a symbiotic phase followed by a separation-individuation phase of between 18 and 36 months useful in understanding the borderline syndrome in adolescents.[73] He studied and treated a number of troubled adolescents who had in common the fact that they had been unable to achieve ego autonomy and a satisfactory psychological separation from their mothers. They suffered from intense feelings of abandonment, which Masterson noted was created by the mother's withdrawal of love and caring when the patient attempted to separate and "individuate."

Mahler herself has tried to observe the possible precursors in infancy of the borderline features of adult personality development.[71] She suggests that the rapidly alternating clinging observed in some small children during the "rapprochement subphase" of separation-individuation may reflect "the fact that the child has split the object world, more permanently than is optimal, into 'good' and 'bad.' By means of this splitting, the 'good' object is defended against the derivatives of the aggressive drive." Mahler suggests that deficiencies of integration and internalization may leave residua and "thus may manifest themselves in borderline mechanisms." Approaching the problem from the direction of the psychoanalysis of adults, Mahler described the case of an unmarried man in his late twenties who suffered from severe mood swings, intense resentment toward those who disappointed him, feelings of abandonment, and feelings of floating away in space. From these and other data of the analysis, Mahler postulated that the patient was fixated to the "rapprochement subphase of development" and split the object world, as in Kernberg's borderline personalities, into "the good symbiotic mother" and "the forbidding 'bad' mother after separation." Although she was able to relate certain borderline phenomena in the psychoanalytic situation to phenomena of the separation-individuation phases of early childhood, Mahler also wrote that she had "come to be more and more convinced that there is no 'direct line' from the deductive use of borderline phenomena to one or another substantive finding of observational research."[71]

Other directions in work in the borderline area can be cited only briefly. The literature continues to grow. The developmental concepts of Mahler and Kernberg have been applied to the study of families of borderline adolescents by a group of investigators at the National Institute of Mental Health. Some of their findings and concepts are presented by John Zinner and Edward R. Shapiro in Chapter 8 of this volume. Gerald Adler and Henry J. Friedman in Boston in separate studies have extended the treatment approaches originally suggested by Knight to hospitalized borderline patients.[5,36] Harold P. Blum has applied psychoanalytic understanding to the handling of regression in borderline patients.[11] Richard D. Chessick has linked the experience of inner deadness and meaninglessness, of which borderline patients complain, to the philosophy of Martin Heidegger, who placed death at the center of life and called the problem of our age "the falling away from Being, or the Being of beings."[19] The debate over nosology continues. Robert Dickes has offered a welcome critique of much of the recent literature on borderline states, but he then disappoints the reader by suggesting a return to the use of Hoch and Polatin's awkward term "pseudoneurotic" coupled with "psychosis, unidentified type" to designate the borderline group.[23]

J. G. Gunderson and M. T. Singer in a review of the relevant descriptive, psychodynamic, and psychological literature pointed out that the description of borderline cases is affected by how the sample is selected, the means whereby data are collected, the context of the observations, and who is doing the describing.[46] They observed that lack of attention to such methodological issues has contributed to the vagueness and confusion in the literature on this subject. Also, inasmuch as the ability to test reality becomes a critical element in the differential diagnosis between borderline and psychotic states, there is a great need for a graded measurable way of assessing this function.

Singer reviewed the findings reported in the psychological literature on the subject of borderlines, which has not been extensive, and also reported on work in which she has been participating.[92] She noted that patients called borderline tend to show good reasoning and appropriate responses on structured tests like the Wechsler-Bellevue, but on unstructured ones like the Rohrschach they may produce even more psychotic and primary process material than to schizophrenics. She distinguished two subgroups of borderline patients in relation to psychological testing—a constricted group, which she likened to David Rapaport's "coarctated" schizophrenics, and a core group, which was prone to give flamboyant or "fabulized" responses with the use of odd expressions, tending to project their own affective ideation onto the Rohrschach test material. The personal presence of the tester would tend to restrain these subjective responses.

George Vaillant, like Elizabeth Zetzel, eschews the term borderline, believing it is more likely to be used to camouflage the patient's character problems than to help appreciate their specific nature.[98] In a promising longitudinal investigative approach, Vaillant had demonstrated the presence of immature defenses, such as projection and acting out, in college students followed over a 30-year period, who later developed normally. Through this work he has raised the question of the relationship of phenomena observed in patients with character problems, or diagnosed "borderline," to the manifestations of everyday life and the struggles of otherwise normal people at various stages of their lives. By implication the important question then becomes not the presence of immature defenses or pathological character traits as such but their quantity (how much they dominate the personality), context (under what circumstances they are used), timing (at what stage of adult life they occur), and immutability.

In summary, the diagnosis of borderline states or character structure has resulted from the confluence of two historical streams. The borderlands of descriptive psychiatry (constituting largely what we would now call the personality disorders) were grouped together around the turn of the century as psychopathic conditions, a term that had a much broader meaning originally than its current connotation of antisocial character would imply. These states stood not so much at the borderline of schizophrenia as at the border of psychiatry. This theme was taken up once again by Chessick in a 1966 paper on borderland patients, who "seem to lie on the periphery of psychiatry, on the periphery of society, and on the periphery of penology."[18]

The second stream was that of psychoanalysis. Psychoanalysts showed an interest in the 1920s and 1930s in applying the evolving dynamic concepts of depth psychology to the understanding of particular character types, but they soon turned their attention to the systematic exploration of the roots and structure of personality and to the development of a theory of object relations. The current interest in borderline conditions reflects a revival of psychoanalytic attention to character pathology, but not so much to its descriptive aspects as to its dynamic features. The borderline states, or patients with borderline personality organization in Kernberg's terminology, constitute a broad group within which there has been little differentiation. They share in common, as Gunderson and his associate Singer have pointed out, disturbances in the areas of emotional expression, control of behavior, social adaptation, and interpersonal relationships.[46] If the patients become psychotic at all, the loss of reality testing is transient and reversible. The borderlines seem to be, in short, a large group of personality disorders, many of whom have been labeled before with other names at a time when the nosology of character types received more attention. It will be recalled that Reich in 1925 called the neurotic character, the impulsive character, and the psychopath "borderline" cases.

REFERENCES

1. Abraham K: Contributions to the theory of the anal character. Int J Psychoanals 4:400–418, 1923. Also in Abraham K: Selected Papers on Psychoanalysis. New York, Basic Books, 1954
2. Abraham K: The influence of oral erotism on character formation. Int J Psychoanal 6:247–258, 1924. Also in Abraham K: Selected Papers on Psychoanalysis. New York, Basic Books, 1954
3. Abraham K: Character formation on the genital level of libido development. Int J Psychoanal 7:214–222, 1926. Also in Abraham K: Selected Papers on Psychoanalysis. New York, Basic Books, 1954
4. Ackerknecht EH: A Short History of Psychiatry. New York, Hafner Publishing, 1959
5. Adler G: Hospital treatment of borderline patients. Amer J Psychiatry 130:32–36, 1973
6. Aichhorn A: Wayward Youth. New York, Meridian Books, 1955
7. Alexander F: The neurotic character. Int J Psychoanal 11:292–313, 1930
8. American Psychiatric Association: Diagnostic and Statistical Manual of Mental Disorders, 2d ed (DSM-II). The Association, 1968
9. Arnstein RL: The borderline patient in the college setting, in Wedge BM (ed): Psychosocial Problems of College Men. New Haven, Yale University Press, 1958, pp 173–199

10. Bleuler E: Textbook of Psychiatry. New York, Dover Publications, 1924
11. Blum HP: Psychoanalytic understanding and psychotherapy of borderline regression. Int J Psychoanal Psychother 1:46–59, 1972
12. Boyer LB, Giovacchini PL: Psychoanalytic Treatment of Schizophrenic and Characterological Disorders. New York, Science House, 1967
13. Burnham JC: Psychoanalysis and American Medicine 1894–1918: Medicine, Science and Culture. New York, International Universities Press, 1967
14. Cary GL: The borderline condition: A structural-dynamic viewpoint. Psychoanal Rev 59(1):33–54, 1972
15. Chase LS: Countertransference in the psychoanalysis of borderline personality disorders. Paper read at the Boston Psychoanalytic Society and Institute, March 23, 1966
16. Chase LS: Discussion of Otto F. Kernberg: Barriers to being in love. Paper read at the Boston Psychoanalytic Society and Institute, March 22, 1972
17. Chase LS, Hire, AW: The borderline character disorder. Unpublished manuscript, 1969
18. Chessick RD: The psychotherapy of borderland patients. Am J Psychother 20:600–614, 1966
19. Chessick RD: Defective ego feeling and the quest for being in the borderline patient. Int J Psychoanal Psychother 3:73–89, 1974
20. Clark PL: Some practical remarks upon the use of modified psychoanalysis in the treatment of borderland neuroses and psychoses. Psychoanal Rev 6:306–308, 1919
21. Coleman ML: Externalization of the toxic introject. A treatment technique for borderline cases. Psychoanal Rev 43:235–242, 1956
22. Deutsch H: Some forms of emotional disturbance and their relationship to schizophrenia. Psychoanal 11:301–321, 1942
23. Dickes R: The concepts of borderline states: An alternative proposal. Int J Psychoanal Psychother 3:1–27, 1974
24. Diefendorf AR: Clinical Psychiatry. Abstracted and adopted from the 7th German edition of Emil Kraepelin's Lehrbuch der Psychiatrie. New York, Macmillan, 1907
25. Eder MD: Borderland medical cases. Universal Medical Record (London) 1914, 5:1–10
26. Eisenstein VW: Differential psychotherapy of borderline states. Psychiatr Qua 25:379–401, 1951
27. Ekstein R, Wallerstein J: Observations on the psychology of borderline and psychotic children: Report from a current psychotherapy research project at Southard School. Psychoanal Study Child 9:344–369, 1954
28. Federn P: Principles of psychotherapy in latent schizophrenia. Am J Psychother 1:129–145, 1947
29. Federn P: Ego Psychology and the Psychoses. New York, Basic Books, 1952

30. Fenichel O: The Psychoanalytic Theory of Neurosis. New York, WW Norton, 1945
31. Foucault M: Madness and Civilization: A History of Insanity in the Age of Reason. New York, Random House, 1965
32. Freud A: The Ego and the Mechanisms of Defense. New York, International Universities Press, 1946
33. Freud S: Character and anal erotism (1908), Standard Edition of the Complete Psychological Works of Sigmund Freud, vol IX. London, Hogarth Press, 1959
34. Freud S: On narcissism: An introduction (1914), Standard Edition of the Complete Psychological Works of Sigmund Freud, vol XIV. London, Hogarth Press, 1957
35. Freud S: Analysis terminable and interminable (1937), Standard Edition of the Complete Psychological Works of Sigmund Freud, vol XXIII. London, Hogarth Press, 1964
36. Friedman HJ: Some problems of in-patient management with borderline patients. Am J Psychiatry 126:47–52, 1969
37. Frijling-Schreuder ECM: Borderline states in children. Psychoanal Study Child 24:307–327, 1969
38. Frosch J: The psychotic character: Clinical psychiatric considerations. Psychiatr Q 38:81–96, 1964
39. Frosch J: Psychoanalytic considerations of the psychotic character. J Am Psychoanal Assoc 18:24–50, 1970
40. Geleerd ER: Borderline states in childhood and adolescence. Psychoanal Study Child 13:279–295, 1958
41. Glover E: A psychoanalytic approach to the classification of mental disorders. J Ment Sci 78:819–842, 1932
42. Glover E: The relation of perversion formation to the development of reality sense. Int J Psychoanal 14: 486–504, 1933
43. Glover E: The criminal psychopath, in Roots of Crime. New York, International Universities Press, 1960, pp. 132–147
44. Grinker RR, Werble B, Drye RC: The Borderline Syndrome. New York, Basic Books, 1968
45. Gunderson J: Paper read at the Annual Meeting of the American Psychiatric Association, Detroit, May 8, 1974
46. Gunderson JG, Singer MT: Defining borderline patients: An overview. Am J Psychiatry 132:1–10, 1975
47. Gunderson J, Carpenter W, Strauss J: Borderline and schizophrenic patients: a comparative study. Unpublished manuscript
48. Havens LL: Some difficulties in giving schizophrenic and borderline patients medication. Psychiatry 31:44–50, 1968
49. Havens LL: Approaches to the Mind. Boston, Little, Brown, 1973
50. Hayman M: Traumatic elements in the analysis of the borderline case. Int J Psychoanal 38:9–21, 1957
51. Hendrick I: Ego development and certain character problems. Psychoanal Q 5:320–346, 1936

52. Hoch PH, Cattell JP: The diagnosis of pseudoneurotic schizophrenia. Psychiatr Q 33:17–43, 1959
53. Hoch PH, Cattell JP, Strahl MO, et al: The course and outcome of pseudoneurotic schizophrenia. Am J Psychiatry 11:106–115, 1962
54. Hoch PH, Polatin P: Pseudoneurotic forms of schizophrenia. Psychiatr Q 23:248–276, 1949
55. Jones E: Anal erotic character traits (1918), in Papers on Psychoanalysis. London, Bailliere, Tindall and Cox, 1950
56. Kaufman I: Some considerations of the "borderline" personality structure and the psychodynamics of the therapeutic process. Smith College Studies in Social Work 26(3):7–17, 1956
57. Kernberg OF: Structural derivatives of object relationships. Int J Psychoanal 47:236–253, 1966
58. Kernberg OF: Borderline personality organization. J Am Psychoanal Assoc 15:641–685, 1967
59. Kernberg OF: A psychoanalytic classification of character pathology. J Am Psychoanal Assoc 18:800–822, 1970
60. Kernberg OF: Barriers to being in love. Paper read at Scientific Meeting at the Boston Psychoanalytic Society and Institute, March 22, 1972. J Am Psychoanal Assoc 22:486–511, 1974
61. Kernberg OF: Further contributions to the treatment of narcissistic personalities. Int J Psychoanal 55:215–240, 1974
62. Klein M: The Psycho-analysis of Children (1932). London, Hogarth Press, 1959
63. Knight RP: Borderline states, in Knight RP, Friedman CR (eds): Psychoanalytic Psychiatry and Psychology, vol I. New York, International Universities Press, 1954, pp 97–109
64. Knight RP: Management and psychotherapy of the borderline schizophrenic patient, in Knight RP, Friedman CR (eds): Psychoanalytic Psychiatry and Psychology, vol I. New York, International Universities Press, 1954, pp 110–122
65. Kohut H: Forms and transformations of narcissism. J Am Psychoanal Assoc 14:243–272, 1966
66. Kut Rosenfeld S, Sprince MP: An attempt to formulate the meaning of the concept "borderline." Psychoanal Study Child 18:603–635, 1963
67. Kut Rosenfeld S, Sprince MP: Some thoughts on the technical handling of borderline children. Psychoanal Study Child 20:495–517, 1965
68. Lazar N: Nature and significance of changes in patients in a psychoanalytic clinic. Psychoanal Q 42:579–600, 1973
69. Lombroso-Ferrero G: Criminal Man, According to the Classification of Cesare Lombroso. New York, G. P. Putnam's Sons, 1911, pp xi–xx, 3–73
70. McCord W, McCord T: The Psychopath. Princeton, Van Nostrand, 1964
71. Mahler MS: A study of the separation individuation process, and its possible application to borderline phenomena in the psychoanalytic situation. Psychoanal Study Child 26:403–425, 1971
72. Malone C: Safety first: Comments on the influence of external danger in

the lives of children of disorganized families. Am J Orthopsychiatry 35:3–12, 1966

73. Masterson J: Treatment of the Borderline Adolescent: A Developmental Approach. New York, Wiley-Interscience, 1972
74. Modell A: Primitive object relations and the predisposition to schizophrenia. Int J Psychoanal 44:282–292, 1963
75. Modell AH: Object Love and Reality. New York, International Universities Press, 1968
76. Modell AH: A narcissistic defense against affects and the illusion of self-suffiency. Talk presented at the Boston Psychoanalytic Society and Institute, October 12, 1974
77. Moore TV: The parataxes: A study and analysis of certain borderline mental states. Psychoanal Rev 8:252–282, 1921
78. Oberndorf CP: The psycho-analysis of border line cases. NY State J Med 30:648–651, 1930
79. Partridge GE: Current conceptions of psychopathic personality. Am J Psychiatry 10:53–99, 1930
80. Pelman C: Psychische Grenzzustande (Extraordinary [or Borderland] States of Mind). Bonn, Von Friedrich Cohen, 1909
81. Pinel P: A Treatise on Insanity. Transl by DD Davis. New York, Hafner Publishing, 1962
82. Prichard JC: A Treatise on Insanity and Other Disorders Affecting the Mind. Philadelphia, Carey an Hart, 1837
83. Rengell L: The borderline case. J Am Psychoanal Assoc 3:285–298, 1955
84. Record of admissions to the Cambridge Hospital (Mass.) Psychiatric In-Patient Service, February–June 1974
85. Reich W: Character Analysis. New York, Orgone Press, 1949
86. Reich W: The Impulsive Character and Other Writings. New York, New American Library, 1974
87. Robbins LL: The borderline case. J Am Psychoanal Assoc 4:550–562, 1956
88. Rolde E: Sociocultural determinants of "character disorder"; a consideration of concepts and direction. MPH Thesis, Harvard School of Public Health, June 1, 1967
89. Schact M, Kempster SW: Useful techniques in the treatment of patients with schizophrenia or borderline states. Psychiatry 16:35–54, 1953
90. Schmideberg M: The treatment of psychopathic and borderline patients. Am J Psychother 1:45–71, 1947
91. Schmideberg M: The borderline patient, in Arieti S (ed): American Handbook of Psychiatry, vol I. New York, Basic Books, 1959, pp 398–416
92. Singer MT: Paper read at the Annual Meeting of the American Psychiatric Association, Detroit, May 8, 1974
93. Stern A: Psychoanalytic investigation of therapy in the border line neuroses. Psychoanal Q 7:467–489, 1938
94. Stern A: Psychoanalytic therapy in the borderline neuroses. Psychoanal Q 14:190–198, 1945

95. Stern A: Transference in borderline neuroses. Psychoanal Q 17:527–528, 1948
96. Stern A: The transference in the borderline group of neuroses. J Am Psychoanal Assoc 5:348–350, 1957
97. Tartakoff H: The normal personality in our culture and the Nobel Prize complex, in Loewenstein RM, et al (eds): Psychoanalysis: A General Psychology. New York, International Universities Press, 1966
98. Vaillant G: Five ego mechanisms underlying character disorders or wisdom is never having to call a patient borderline. Talk presented at Cambridge Hospital (Mass.), September 23, 1974
99. Weinberger J: Basic concepts in diagnosis and treatment of borderline states. Smith College Studies in Social Work 26(2):18–23, 1956
100. Weiner B: Psychodiagnosis in Schizophrenia. New York, John Wiley, 1966
101. Werble B: Second follow-up study of borderline patients. Arch Gen Psychiatry 23:3–7, 1970
102. Winkelstein C: Psychotherapy of the borderline schizophrenic with heroin addiction. J Hillside Hospital (Long Island, New York) 5:78–90, 1956
103. Wolberg AR: The "borderline" patient. Am J Psychother 6:694–710, 1952
104. Wolberg AR: The Borderline Patient. New York, Intercontinental Medical Book, 1973
105. Zetzel ER: The so-called good hysteric. Int J Psychoanal 49:256–260, 1968
106. Zilboorg G: Ambulatory schizophrenias. Psychiatry 4:149–155, 1941
107. Zilboorg G: The problem of ambulatory schizophrenias. J Am Psychiatry 113:519–525, 1956
108. Zilboorg G: Further observations on ambulatory schizophrenias. Am J Orthopsychiatry 27:677–682, 1957

Gerald Adler

2

The Usefulness of the "Borderline" Concept in Psychotherapy

Gerald Adler belongs to the group of psychoanalysts and therapists who believe in the specificity and usefulness of the borderline concept. He designates as borderline cases patients with stable character structures who demonstrate the immature defenses stressed by Otto F. Kernberg— splitting, primitive idealization, projection, and projective identification—and the core conflicts related to primitive hostility and fear of abandonment. Adler's borderline patients suffer from severe disturbances in human relationships, especially those that require closeness on a one-to-one basis. A disturbance in the mother–child relationship in Margaret Mahler's separation-individuation phase is postulated.

The therapeutic strategies suggested by Adler are derived from an understanding of the patient's defensive organization and his conflicts in the formation of object relationships. In dealing with the patient the therapist must offer himself as both a supportive person and a figure for identification. The patient learns especially to identify with the way that the therapist cares about him, thereby overcoming the fear of closeness inspired by the early perception of the parental figures as menacing or rejecting.

Since the 1960s the psychiatric and psychoanalytic literature about the borderline patient has been expanding rapidly. The contributions during this period have slowly helped accomplish a decisive step: the concept of the "borderline" patient has become increasingly better defined and thus

I wish to thank Dan H. Buie, Jr., M.D., and Paul G. Myerson, M.D., for help in the preparation of this manuscript.

useful to the clinician. It no longer is a catch-all label for an ill-defined category of patients who fall somewhere between psychosis and neurosis.

When we state that a patient has a borderline personality organization,[13] we are making not only a diagnosis but also a prediction of significant clinical and psychotherapeutic import. We are defining a patient who has many "higher level" strengths, including defenses, but who in specific ways is vulnerable within dyadic relationships. The stresses that can occur within important dyadic relationships can elicit regressions to certain primitive feelings, behaviors, and defenses; if the stress is sufficiently great, the patient may become transiently psychotic. However, psychotic episodes are usually short-lived and specifically related to excessive tension arising within the dyadic situation. Psychotherapy for these patients will often lead to some repetition of the stressful feelings. The relationship with the therapist is often the stimulus that may bring forth what will be described here as the life-and-death struggles that these patients attempt to master. When these issues emerge in the transference, the therapist can anticipate specific difficulties in alliance formation and a tendency for a tenuous working alliance to break down repeatedly. The regressions of these patients, which are in part the reexperiencing of unresolved problems early in life, provide the opportunity for the therapist to use his clinical and theoretical understanding to help repair specific defects and maladaptive responses. The therapist will face certain specific countertransference issues within himself as he attempts this work.

Otto F. Kernberg's contributions[13-15] defining borderline personality organization provide the clearest descriptions about a group of patients who have stable character structures but who can shift transiently into psychosis with sufficiently severe stress. John Frosch's valuable papers on the psychotic character[9, 10] define a similar group of patients with stable personality characteristics whose reality testing remains relatively intact except during stress. Both Kernberg and Frosch are describing the same group of patients, but they emphasize different aspects of them based on their clinical and theoretical points of view. Frosch's clarifications about defects in reality sense and reality testing in these patients are discussed by Kernberg in the context of their primitive defenses and in the framework of object-relations theory.

Kernberg bases the diagnosis of borderline personality organization on a constellation of symptoms, defenses, and specific aspects of ego strength or weakness as well as on a developmental history.[13] He stresses the "lower level" defenses of these patients, i.e., the defenses that derive from the early years of life at a time when clear distinctions between child and parent were first solidifying and the child was attempting to synthesize positive and negative feelings about the same person. His writings draw upon the contributions of Melanie Klein, Edith Jacobson, W. Ronald D. Fairbairn, Harry Guntrip, and Donald W. Winnicott.

Borderline patients tend to feel very needy within relationships, and they quickly develop the belief that their life literally depends upon the existence and support of another human being—very much as the infant and the very small child do. These patients utilize corresponding defenses derived from that early period of childhood, e.g., splitting, primitive idealization, projection, and projective identification. It is important to reemphasize that they also have "higher level" defenses (i.e., neurotic defenses) and possess the good reality testing capacities that accompany them. However, borderline patients regress to their primitive repertory under the stress of their wishes and needs that arise within important relationships. The regression is often accompanied by vivid fantasies of extreme neediness, destruction, and abandonment. Many of the patients simultaneously preserve areas of good functioning, such as a capacity to work in a career.

Some authors, including Heinz Kohut,[16] distinguish between borderline patients and narcissistic patients, based in part on the latter's capacity to be productive in work and maintain areas of achievement even though there may be serious limitations in their creativity. Kohut also defines aspects of the transference manifestations of the narcissistic character, e.g., mirror and idealizing transferences. However, these elements are also present in borderlines, but not in the pure culture found in narcissistic characters, i.e., borderline patients are much more likely to regress from these narcissistic transferences to the hungry, demanding, clinging state when their longings are not met.

Though Kernberg's writings present the clearest descriptive, structural, and dynamic statement about borderline patients, they leave somewhat ambiguous the varieties of styles in which these patients can relate to others. When most mental health professionals in the United States discuss borderline patients, they, as Kernberg, seem to be talking about persons who rapidly involve themselves in intense, clinging, demanding relationships while fearing mutual destructiveness, rejection, and abandonment within these relationships. They seem to be describing patients sometimes called primitive or oral hysterics—patients who sexualize relationships and long for their devouring hunger and wishes to merge, but are terrified of this happening. When English writers, such as Guntrip,[12] talk about borderlines, they seem to include patients who might ordinarily be labeled schizoid in the United States. These "schizoid" patients have the same core conflicts as the flamboyant, clinging borderlines, i.e., the life-and-death, devour or be devoured issues. However, as part of their character style, they choose withdrawal and isolation as a way of attempting to cope with these wishes. Donald L. Burnham and his associates describe similar wishes and fears as they are experienced by schizophrenics as the "need-fear dilemma." Guntrip[12] graphically presents the dream of a patient who attempted to control the helpless, infantile desperate part of herself; in her dream she sees a tiny naked infant with wide-open expressionless eyes locked inside of a steel filing cabinet.

The warding-off, rejecting, disdainful attitude that these patients often convey is an attempt to convince themselves and others that their desperate, helpless crying part is nonexistent. In contrast, the more flamboyant clinging patients are more likely to have dreams in which their fragile shells can be or actually are crushed and destroyed. But both groups of patients share identical core issues. In addition, there are patients who present both pictures, alternating between a desperate clinging and an aloof indifference.

We are seeing in our offices and psychiatric hospital units a series of patients with the same borderline personality disorders involving many of the same primitive defenses. Therefore, it seems useful to view these patients as a continuum belonging to one group that pose similar treatment issues, experience similar transference phenomena, and arouse similar countertransference fantasies and difficulties in their therapists. The differences in working with the patients in the group are related to the vicissitudes, on the one hand, of working with a patient who tends to overwhelm the therapist with the intensity of his responses to the therapist, and, on the other hand, of working with someone who maintains an extreme distance because of his fear of such involvement.

The borderline patient in his daily existence attempts to cope with one repeated fear and conviction—that he has been and will be abandoned by important people in his life.[1,2,5] The histories of borderline patients always reveal real loss, relative neglect, or overindulgence alternating with neglect. Sometimes one can document one or a series of traumatic events at one and one-half years of age to two and one-half years. This period is a particularly vulnerable one for normal development since it is the time when a child first tenuously establishes the capacity to evoke the memory of someone who is not present:[8] he still needs his mother to reaffirm that he has a secure responsive parent.[19,20] When his separation anxiety mounts, this newly established memory capacity is in danger of breaking down. Since newly achieved capacities are extremely vulnerable,[16] a failure of adequate mothering at this time can lead to a regression to an earlier period in which the child feels that his life literally depends upon the existence and continued presence of another person.

Accompanying the regression are feelings of rejection and fears of abandonment.

The borderline patient's conviction that he will ultimately be rejected also derives from another aspect of his conviction about himself; he feels that he is a destructively angry person who deserves capital punishment and rejection.[5] His anger occurs in the form of a very primitive, infantile, all-or-nothing murderous rage, which is akin to that of the small child who feels that he desperately needs feeding, holding, touching, warmth, and comforting in order to survive but does not see it forthcoming. This anger, therefore, is a secondary phenomenon, occurring in response to the patient's feeling that his survival needs will not be adequately met. This experience derives from a period in which a thought and action are the same to the small child and occurs developmentally at a time when he has an archaic superego that is readily projected and can be experienced in the form of someone who can punish the child viciously for such destructive fantasies.

A borderline patient lacks the ability to maintain an image of good interactions with important people in his life. He may not think about the important person at all, or he may find himself continuously preoccupied with thoughts about that person. But at moments of stress, particularly precipitated by rage at that person for not fulfilling an intense need, the vitally important capacity to feel that the person is with him in a caring way can disappear, resulting in a sense of utter aloneness, helplessness, panic, and, ultimately, despair. One patient described her fury at not receiving an adequate response from an important person in terms of picturing herself stomping on that person until he was dead. She then felt empty, desperate, and alone, with an impenetrable wall around her. Clearly, such a patient cannot tolerate angry feelings toward important people and is particularly prone to experiencing increasing difficulties in therapy when angry feelings inevitably arise toward the therapist. As described above, this phenomenon appears to be similar to the two-year-old's tenuously established capacity to internalize an object: it can be too readily lost during the frustrations arising from inadequate mothering.

The borderline patient experiences intense longings but often finds himself receiving little satisfaction of these longings. In part, this can be the result of the rejection he provokes because of his inevitably escalating demands. It can also follow because he seeks distant, aloof people to associate with and chooses relative isolation in order to protect himself from his devouring, destructive wishes that he fears will emerge in relationships. Observations during the treatment of one patient gave some clues to this problem. When she finally achieved the capacity to go out on dates, she felt desperate; she felt that the "boys" she met were uncommitted to her and rejecting when she was feeling so helplessly needy with them. As she became able to separate her demands and projections from the real qualities of these men, it became apparent that they were passive, inhibited, obsessional people who were frightened by involvement with women, especially someone as demanding as this patient. Gradually she became able to control the intensity of her demands; finally she became involved in a relationship in which a warm man fell in love with her and pursued her for herself, specifically for the healthy aspects of her personality. Her response was one of terror, a sense of being smothered, and a conviction that the man was weak, helpless, and ineffectual (as she often described herself). She also felt a murderous rage, with wishes to tear at him and strangle him. Thus, her attempt to accept a genuinely warm relationship evoked her fears of fusion, a transient breakdown of ego boundaries, and a massive use of projective identification, i.e., placing her intolerable feelings into someone else who then must be controlled.[13] It readily became understandable why she had previously chosen the uncommitted, distant, obsessional man.

This discussion of the characteristics, dynamics, and early background of the borderline patient can be utilized in defining a therapeutic approach that can anticipate certain specific difficulties that are likely to occur in a patient–therapist relationship. Winnicott's concept of the "good-enough mother"[23] can be adapted as a basic framework in which to discuss psychotherapy with borderline patients. Winnicott has described the difficulties of the small child who will have severe problems later in life. He defined the mother–child relationship of such a child as one in which the mother is too often incapable of responding adequately to the needs of her child. Her failure is a relative one and involves a relative lack of empathy with the frequently varying needs and demands of her child. The child's rage, helplessness, and despair are secondary to his experiences of an inadequate maternal "holding" environment.

No matter what other characteristics, skills, and goals that he possesses, a therapist treating borderline patients must have the capacity to be empathically in touch with his patient in a way that can offer the patient the opportunity to repair to some degree the early experiences of inadequate mothering. We can define this therapist as the "good-enough therapist,"[6]—i.e., he is not perfect, but more often than not he is in tune with his patient's varying and complex needs and responds with a sufficient combination of understanding, support, and necessary deprivation to help his patient grow optimally. Although the therapist may become angry, helpless, and despairing at times as he works with his patients,[1–3] his efforts, consciously and unconsciously, are to help the patient, despite whatever sadism and depression he may feel in response to his patient.[4] Within the context of the good-enough therapist it becomes possible to define certain specific therapeutic issues that can be expected to arise in therapy with borderline patients.

As already described, the borderline patient enters any interpersonal situation, including therapy, feeling that he is bad and worthless and can expect rejection. At the same time he feels intense needs in order to survive. These overwhelming needs, following a loss or disappointment, are what may lead him to a therapist's office for help. However, he has minimal capacity to modulate the intensity of his needs and feelings as they come up in a dyadic relationship such as psychotherapy. The good-enough therapist has an intellectual and empathic grasp of these borderline issues. In addition, he is aware of the tenuous balance in a borderline patient between his sense of having someone empathically in tune with him and the disorganizing experience of his rage when he feels excessively deprived or misunderstood. Particularly early in treatment, before any significant relationship or tentative alliance is formed, a borderline patient is particularly likely to feel abandoned and rejected by the therapist who is not aware of this delicate equilibrium. The degree of activity of the therapist often becomes the matrix of the "holding" necessary for the patient to maintain a shaky, but sufficient sense of integrity. This therapeutic activity includes questions, clarifications, and definitions of the work to be done together. Sometimes the therapist may speak, not so much to make a clarification or effect some other therapeutic maneuver, but because he senses that his silence or lack of activity at that moment arouses more anxiety or anger secondary to the feelings of abandonment than the patient can bear.

The therapist always needs to assess carefully the adequacy of his activity. Did the patient become more comfortable, or did he feel smothered? Was he promised an ultimate gratification that could never be forthcoming, or did he feel that the therapist was too aloof and uninterested? Since the patient brings these concerns, as well as his primitive and brittle defenses into treatment immediately, the sensitivity and adequacy of the good-enough therapist's responses help the patient maintain a better balance between the intense extremes of his needs and fears. The therapist's assessment that he is working with a borderline patient alerts him to this kind of responsiveness and sensitivity. This is a must if he is to help his patient become comfortable enough to begin to look at some of the issues in his life that brought him to the therapist.

More papers have been appearing in the literature about the need for the therapist to be "real" when he treats the borderline patient, i.e., be willing to reveal openly certain aspects of himself and his life. These papers sometimes miss the essence of the issue—i.e., it is the *quality* of therapist activity rather than the extent of the therapist's self-revelation that is required by the patient in order to feel the holding, support, and concern of his therapist instead of a sense of abandonment and rejection. Ralph R. Greenson[11] has demonstrated the significant difference between silence in response to a patient's question and the therapist's explanation about the reasons that he may choose not to answer a question. The therapist's silence, which may sometimes impede the therapy and the formation of a working alliance with a neurotic patient, can be a devastating experience for the borderline. For some borderline patients the activity of the therapist may have to include sharing a few details about the therapist's life; the decision is based on the needs of the patient, among which may be the necessity to clarify certain doubts and fantasies about the therapist. Whether and how the therapist provides answers, including personal information, has to be based on his empathic awareness of the patient's need for this activity as well as his awareness of when a clarification of reality would be useful for a patient who has such a tenuous capacity to test reality when under stress. He also has to assess whether a specific response will enhance the patient's comfort and will support the tentative alliance or whether it will frighten the patient with too much closeness. The therapist may find that he can explain to the patient why it may or may not be useful to have certain questions answered. He may even be able to enlist the patient's aid to decide whether a certain answer or piece of information should be supplied.

Sometimes the reasons given in clinical discussions for a therapist to reveal the details of his life and personal values include the statement that the patient's knowledge of the therapist provides a model for identification. In my opinion a patient does not identify with the facts of a therapist's life; rather he identifies with the way that the therapist cares about him and is sensitive to his varying needs and with the way that the therapist masters his own anxiety as he is confronted by the often intense life-and-death issues, affects, and demands of his patient. Every therapist, by the fact of his physical presence, reveals much about himself, even though a patient never requests a single "fact" about his life or may even complain that he knows nothing about him.

Since all borderline patients possess a limited capacity to form a working or therapeutic alliance, the therapist must always evaluate whether any intervention supports or weakens this alliance. The good-enough therapist recognizes the ease with which the tentative alliance can break down when the patient feels abandoned and angry. On the other hand, the therapist knows that his ultimate task is to help his patient learn to bear this sense of rejection and rage and put it into perspective. The task is particularly difficult in the borderline group of patients because they can fluctuate rapidly between a feeling of some alliance with the therapist and a furious, overwhelming feeling of isolation and emptiness.

The therapist also knows that borderline patients lack a well-developed capacity to stand back and observe their interactions with people and their thoughts and fantasies. They are much too prone to see themselves in terms of total badness rather than to conceptualize that they are people with problems. Their tenuous sense of self easily fragments under the stress of feelings of abandonment and rage. The splitting processes that occur under these circumstances leave them experiencing their badness as all there is that exists within them at the moment. The good-enough therapist is aware of this regressive propensity and attempts to offer enough support to avoid unnecessary experiences that his borderline patient can only interpret as rejection. When the patient is ready to bear it, the therapist is also able to allow his patient to feel and verbalize the experience of abandonment and rage. The therapist also learns to address his comments to his patient in a way that always supports the idea of two people working together to observe and understand.

The longing that a borderline patient has for a close, warm, holding relationship also frightens him because of the rapidity with which it can threaten his capacity to maintain his sense of separateness within relationships. In therapy, a borderline patient is terrified of this possibility even though he simultaneously wishes and demands so much closeness, a demand that he often expects the therapist to fulfill magically. The work of therapy ultimately involves helping the patient to understand and resolve this dilemma. However, in order for this work to proceed, the patient needs to feel that his tenuous autonomy is respected and nurtured, even though his demands at that moment may be for exactly the opposite experience. The therapeutic approach that emphasizes the collaborative nature of the work and the patient's gradual acquisition of capacities to observe, conceptualize, and understand is one that supports this developing autonomy. The more the therapist can help the patient assume increasing responsibility within the bounds of a supportive relationship, the more the patient can feel safe from his fear of loss of ego boundaries. This approach also emphasizes the various choices that the patient has at any specific point of time in his life and helps him utilize the therapist in making these choices. Again, this approach must often be maintained in the face of demands for magically correct answers. The therapist's task consists of providing enough support so that the patient does not feel abandoned, yet allowing sufficient autonomy so that the patient does not feel forced or coerced. When the therapist maintains this balance with sensitivity, he also implicitly shows his patient that he does not possess the magical omnipotent powers that the patient ascribes to him. He, however, does not force the patient to give up this narcissistic, idealizing image of his therapist as long as it is a crucial and sustaining part of the transference.[16]

This discussion of the borderline patient's tenuous ability to maintain a working alliance, his limited capacity to observe and sustain a stable therapeutic distance, and his brittle defenses implies the need for the therapist to supply structure, reality testing, and limit setting. The approach described in these pages emphasizes that alliance formation and respect for the patient's autonomy automatically provides this structure. However, the regressive wishes that can emerge in the transference can stress this therapeutically supplied structure and require the therapist to define the realistic limits of his ability to work with his patient.[2-4] In this situation it is important that the therapist not respond in a deleterious manner to the rage and provocativeness that these patients can unleash with excruciating intensity.

Work with borderline patients places a serious responsibility on therapists to maintain the capacities within themselves that they wish to help their patients eventually develop. It requires constant vigilance on the part of therapists not to regress in the face of the intense transference feelings of these patients. Borderline patients, because of their intense wishes and fears, and their primitive defenses, tend to get themselves and their therapists into "all-or-nothing" positions. Their extreme need may arouse rescuing responses from their therapists, which may make the patients feel engulfed and smothered. Or their aloofness and distancing defenses may lead their therapists to experience boredom and a tendency to withdraw or retaliate.

The good-enough therapist's concern especially centers around his potential destructiveness in response to his patient's devaluations and murderous attacks and provocations. Just as with the good-enough mother, the therapist's constructive mastery over his own sadism and fury helps maintain the balance of his responses on the side of helping his patient grow. Loss of this balance can lead to the therapist's retaliation or withdrawal when his patient attacks or devalues,[1,4] or can lead to the therapist's helplessness and despair in response to his patient's repeated need to destroy whatever the therapist tries to offer.[2] The success of the good-enough therapist's attempts to observe and monitor his own fantasies and responses is an important factor in determining whether he can allow his patient to grow and permit the separation-individuation process to occur as part of the therapeutic process[19,20] or whether he has to hang onto the gratification of mother–child fusion that a borderline patient needs earlier in treatment.[4]

Since borderline patients also possess significant "higher level" defenses and functioning, the regressive experiences that can arise in psychotherapy—the life-and-death issues as well as the use of projection and projective identification—can provoke therapists to view these patients as "bad" and willfully misbehaving during a regression and respond to them in punitive, rejecting ways.[3] The therapist who works effectively with a borderline patient understands that a borderline patient can elicit primitive but usually submerged elements within the therapist that are similar to those of the patient's. The therapist's burden includes learning to be able to accept these primitive aspects of himself and to use them to assess the patient's concerns and fantasies as well as to check his own potential destructiveness.[21,22]

Therapeutic growth for a borderline patient involves (1) elements of a corrective emotional experience with a new, consistent, caring nonretaliatory object; (2) experiences with the therapist in which the patient discovers that he cannot destroy this new object; (3) the acquisition of an understanding of the pathological processes that allows the patient to view in perspective his current relationships, his past, and the transference; and (4) ultimately, growth through the higher level preoedipal and oedipal conflicts in a manner similar to that of neurotic patients who begin their therapeutic work there.

REFERENCES

1. Adler G: Valuing and devaluing in the psychotherapeutic process. Arch Gen Psychiatry 22:454–461, 1970
2. Adler G: Helplessness in the helpers. Br J Med Psychol 45:315–326, 1972
3. Adler G: Hospital treatment of borderline patients. Am J Psychiatry 130:32–36, 1973
4. Adler G, Buie DH Jr: The misuses of confrontation with borderline patients. Int J Psychoanal Psychother 1:109–120, 1972
5. Buie DH Jr, Adler G: The uses of confrontation with borderline patients. Int J Psychoanal Psychother 1:90–108, 1972
6. Buie DH Jr: Personal communication. 1972
7. Burnham DL, Gladstone AI, Gibson RW: Schizophrenia and the Need-Fear Dilemma. New York, International Universities Press, 1969
8. Fraiberg S: Libidinal object constancy and mental representation. Psychoanal Study Child 24:9–47, 1969
9. Frosch J: The psychotic character: Clinical psychiatric considerations. Psychiatr Q 38:81–96, 1964
10. Frosch J: Psychoanalytic considerations of the psychotic character. J Am Psychoanal Assoc 18:24–50, 1970
11. Greenson RR: The Technique and Practice of Psychoanalysis, vol I. New York, International Universities Press, 1967, pp 199–201

12. Guntrip H: Psychoanalytic Theory, Therapy, and the Self. New York, Basic Books, 1971
13. Kernberg OF: Borderline personality organization. J Am Psychoanal Assoc 15:641–685, 1967
14. Kernberg OF: The treatment of patients with borderline personality organization. Int J Psychoanal 49:600–619, 1968
15. Kernberg OF: A psychoanalytic classification of character pathology. J Am Psychoanal Assoc 18:800–822, 1970
16. Kohut H: The psychoanalytic treatment of narcissistic personality disorders. Psychoanalytic Study Child 23:86–113, 1968
17. Kohut H: The Analysis of the Self. New York, International Universities Press, 1971
18. Kohut H: Thoughts on narcissism and narcissistic rage. Psychoanal Study Child 27:360–400, 1972
19. Mahler MS: A study of the separation-individuation process: And its possible application to borderline phenomena in the psychoanalytic situation. Psychoanal Study Child. 26:403–424, 1971
20. Mahler MS: Rapprochement subphase of the separation-individuation process. Psychoanal Q 41:487–506, 1972
21. Maltsberger JT, Buie DH Jr: Countertransference hate in the treatment of suicidal patients. Arch Gen Psychiatry 30:625–633, 1974
22. Winnicott DW: Hate in the countertransference. Int J Psychoanal 30:69–75, 1949
23. Winnicott DW: Ego distortion in terms of true and false self, in The Maturational Processes and the Facilitating Environment. New York, International Universities Press, 1965, pp 140–152

Howard A. Wishnie

3

Inpatient Therapy with Borderline Patients

The label "borderline" tends to be applied in inpatient settings (sometimes pejoratively) to nonpsychotic individuals whose lives are in turmoil and whose readiness to translate feelings into impulsive action disrupts the functioning of a hospital ward. Such patients require constant setting of effective limits. (They also remind one of Wilhelm Reich's impulsive character.) Hospitalization is often precipitated by the threat or danger of suicide and occurs most often at a time of crisis in a patient's experience with other persons upon whom he has become dependent.

In the hospital so-called borderline patients recapitulate in their involvement with the ward staff the patterns of interaction that they have employed in relationships in the family and in the community. The period of hospitalization, ideally quite brief, may be used to provide a caring but structured human environment in which the patient can learn to tolerate his feelings without resorting to destructive or maladaptive action and behavior. Hospitalization may be the starting point in the formation of human ties that are more trusting and less exploitative than those of the past.

Howard A. Wishnie writes from his experience as a psychiatrist working in inpatient settings with patients who are designated as borderline.

This chapter examines some of the difficulties of work with the borderline patient from the standpoint of an intensive treatment-oriented psychiatric ward. It is divided into several areas and focuses upon (1) the early diagnosis of the patient and definition of treatment objectives by patient and staff, (2) the staff problems in dealing with patients whose actions reflect some of their own repressed wishes, and (3) finally the treatment objectives of hospitalization in the context of long-term treatment of the patient with the borderline personality.

THE INPATIENT MANAGEMENT
OF THE BORDERLINE PATIENT

Many of the difficulties of inpatient work with borderline patients have been outlined by Henry J. Friedman[3] and Gerald Adler.[1] Both authors found that an intensive treatment setting seemed to promote regression and self-destructive acting out by these patients unless behavioral limits were defined clearly and early in the hospitalization. There was a marked contrast between the rapid regression of patients within the hospital and their prehospitalization state of relatively stable pathology. When these patients became so regressed that they were unmanageable in the intensive treatment milieu, transfer to a minimal treatment, custodial state hospital was followed by rapid reconstruction and discharge. At other times immediate discharge into the community, even in the midst of apparent regression, appeared to promote rapid reconstitution to the level of premorbid functioning.

This author has had the opportunity to observe and confirm both Friedman's and Adler's findings in four different settings: a psychodynamically oriented long-term treatment center, a behavioral-therapy-oriented psychiatric service, a general hospital psychiatry service, and an open-door, prisonlike treatment center for male addicts with criminal histories. Although the settings were oriented differently in terms of treatment modalities used, patients with borderline personality organization responded similarly to hospitalization. Rapid infantile regression and dependence on the staff was followed by destructive rage when the wish for immediate relief of distress did not occur. Arnold H. Modell[9] discusses this reaction in terms of the individual's relationship with his therapist: "The therapist is perceived invariably as one endowed with magical, omnipotent qualities, who will, merely by his contact with a patient, affect a cure without the necessity of the patient to be active or responsible."[8] In terms of Modell's description, the hospital provides many such potential therapists. Each person (nurse, aide, resident, student, and the like) by virtue of his general designation as a "helper" becomes a potential source of the magical relief and also a potential trigger for the rage-filled disappointment. Thus, the very structure of an intensive treatment setting contains the elements for destructive regression.

If one accepts the foregoing, it raises the question of the value of a treatment-oriented, noncustodial hospitalization. The purpose of this discussion is to define the potential usefulness of treatment-oriented inpatient hospitalization. For hospitalization to be of value, several factors are necessary:

1. Rapid identification of the patient as having a borderline personality organization.
2. Clear definition of goals, limits, and expectations of the hospitalization (stabilization of patient).
3. Education of the staff in terms of consistent responses and interactions with these patients (stabilization of the staff).

DIAGNOSIS

The diagnosis of a person having a borderline personality organization is of major importance to the patient and the staff who will be working with the individual. Treatment based upon misdiagnosis can lead to regressive responses in the patient. The following example illustrates the necessity for early diagnosis:

Mr. A.B. was a 20-year-old college dropout at the time of admission. During high school he had been an articulate, intelligent student who appeared to conform to the conservative standards of his home and school. He entered a college that was philosophically liberal and organized in an unstructured fashion. Within several weeks after his first semester began, the patient had drastically altered his modes of speech, dress, and hygiene. Concomitantly he began experimenting with drugs, heterosexual and homosexual relationships. The intensity of this behavior escalated throughout the school year. By the end of his second semester the patient had become withdrawn and suspicious of the people about him. He then returned to his home where he stayed in bed for two months.

After this period the patient entered a psychiatric hospital where he underwent a three-month evaluation period. He later described this hospitalization as the best time in his life. As he saw it, all of his needs were met and he could spend his time writing and illustrating a book of hallucinations and delusions. The more he wrote, the more attention he felt he received—and the more he tended to hallucinate.

At the end of his evaluation the family and patient were given to understand that he was suffering from schizophrenia and would require three to five years of intensive inpatient hospitalization. As the family could not afford this, they sought psychiatric treatment at several other hospitals. At each new hospital the patient consciously contrived to be discharged within several days because none of the hospitals provided the same intense care as his former hospital.

When the family arrived at the hospital where the author was training, a senior supervisor saw the patient and diagnosed his situation as a severe regression within the context of a borderline personality organization. The patient reluctantly admitted himself to the day center. It was expected that he would return home each night and weekend and be responsible for his behavior in the interim time. (The patient initially demanded longterm inpatient treatment. "What do I have to do to show you that I need 24-hour care?")

Within ten days the patient was traveling back and forth to the hospital via public transportation. He complained of visual hallucinations on his trips to and from the hospital. When it was pointed out that he was able to arrive each day and return home in spite of these frightening experiences, the hallucinations diminished and subsequently disappeared. In numerous circumstances the same chain of events occurred. The patient would reluctantly accept responsibility for a particular piece of behavior, become anxious, and develop symptoms that he loudly elaborated. Each time, however, he was able to see that in spite of anxiety and manifest symptoms he was able to accomplish his task.

Within two months he was discharged to outpatient therapy, and he returned to a different college the following September. During the two-year period of follow-up, he remained in school and was successful both academically and socially. He did not undergo further psychotic regressions or require hospitalization.

This example does not imply that the patient's character was altered, nor does it describe the turmoil of his therapy. It is presented in order to demonstrate that early diagnosis and appropriately structured therapy are of major importance to the person with a borderline personality. Because of the importance of identification, several of the many modes of presentation will be discussed in this chapter.

MODES OF PRESENTATION

Depression

The borderline patient who seeks hospitalization prior to self-destructive action will frequently complain of a sense of depression and anxiety. Usually there is a history of chronic, almost timeless, loss and despair. It is difficult for the patient to pinpoint a specific turning point. Careful questioning may reveal relatively stable functioning until a recent period. The patient tends to discount the evidence of recent well-being as inconsequential. He seems to become immersed in the abysmal details of his tragic circumstances. Frequently during the interview, the patient's behavior and expression change to match the content of his history. It is as if he is physically attempting to communicate and convince one of the utter desolation of his life. In spite of, or because of, this the evaluator may feel compelled to act to rescue the patient. His usual professional reserve or judgment is bent or discarded. The evaluator may note overly strong feelings of attachment and concern for the patient that are unusual upon such brief acquaintance.

In spite of the patient's despairing and depressed countenence, a person with a borderline personality communicates a sense of energy and a capacity to engage the therapist quickly. Such a response, coupled with a history of multiple life changes (jobs, career goals, interests, relationships) and impulsive behavior that seem markedly out of character with the patient's current status, should alert one to the possibility that the patient has a borderline character structure.

Postregression: Without Manifest Anxiety

Many patients are seen after a chaotic and self-destructive episode. This may take the form of an overdose, an alcoholic or sexual binge, an episode of self-mutilation, or a struggle with civil authorities. In spite of the patient's injured physical state, he evinces little overt anxiety, depression, embarrassment, or interest in his physical status. Attempts to discuss the episode may bring forth a bland matter-of-fact description or a frank statement that the episode is over and that there is little to be gained in reviewing it.

Unlike many patients who are deferential in response to physicians and medical professionals, borderline patients may have an attitude of anger, entitlement, and haughty disdain. One such patient refused to have a doctor suture self-inflicted lacerations because she did not like his manner. Although the medical staff was concerned about the bleeding and possible permanent damage, the patient ignored all of these dangers. Another patient presented the author with seriously lacerated and bleeding wrists and said angrily, "Sew them up; if you had been here, this wouldn't have happened."

The borderline patient undergoes object-related crises and regressions (note the last-mentioned quote). When the regression has served the purpose of restoring the lost object or a new substitute object, the patient regains his equilibrium and then experiences little overt distress.

Postregression: Sulking

Some borderline patients are seen following suicidal gestures* and appear to be angrily sulking. When initially seen, such patients are silent, hostile, and withdrawn. They complain that they are failures at every-

---

*Suicidal gestures are defined here as attempts at self-destruction that, if carried out to their fullest extent, would not result in death.

thing, even suicide. These individuals may precipitate angry struggles with the staff by being sullen, negativistic, and uncooperative. At the same time they may appear to be friendly and outgoing with other patients or a few selected staff members.

The mood of these patients reflects the fact that the impulsive behavior did not immediately restore to them the lost object. However, within several hours of hospitalization these patients are usually brighter and more cheerful. In examining the change in mood of such a patient, one usually finds that the patient has formed new and intense relationships with the staff and patient community. These new relationships have replaced the lost ones. At the same time lost objects (parents, lovers, friends) may have reestablished contact with the patient.

The Suicidally Determined Patient with No Overt Depression or Psychosis

The borderline patient, with a suicidal bent but presenting no overt depression, enters an emergency room or consultation room in a businesslike manner. The appearance is usually neat and organized. The patient will speak of his current life situation as being chaotic, depressing, and hopeless. In spite of the history that the patient presents, there is little overt evidence of depression. The therapist senses both determination, energy, and a lack of any sense of responsibility on the part of the patient for his own well-being. As one patient stated, "I am going to kill myself, and it's up to you to see that I don't." Another patient called her therapist while he was hospitalized for surgery and said, "If you can't give me a reason to live, right now, I am going to kill myself."

Some understanding of this mode of presentation is presented by Modell in his clarification of some of the dynamic underpinnings of the borderline personality organization: "There is a confusion of the sense of self with the object: and the object is perceived in accordance with certain infantile fantasies concerning the mother. For the picture of the self is regularly composed of two pictures, one, that of a helpless infant, the other that of someone who is omnipotently giving or omnipotently destructive. The patient attributes the omnipotently benevolent or omnipotently destructive aspect of the self-image to the physician. He in turn is left with the feeling that he is nothing but a helpless child."[8] In the clinical example of the patient calling her therapist, the therapist was given the omnipotent position of being responsible for destroying or preserving the patient's life merely by presenting a reason for living.

The lack of direct evidence of clinical depression or psychosis coupled with the clear and demanding quality of the patient frequently has a negative effect on the evaluating physician. At times the seriousness of the patient's intent may be overlooked and there can he disastrous results.

Psychotic Presentation

A borderline patient may undergo brief but dramatic psychotic regressions. These are transient and quickly reversible psychoses that may be classified as schizophrenic, manic, or undifferentiated.[4] The patient presents his symptoms in a flamboyant manner, giving vivid descriptions of auditory or visual hallucinations, or appearing grossly disorganized and confused. If one observes the psychotic presentation, one will note that the quality of this behavior seems to engage many people in the patient's life and becomes yet another form of restitution of the lost objects. Whereas the genuinely schizophrenic patient generally is more discreet and secretive about his hallucinatory or delusional experience, the borderline patient seems to advertise in great detail the psychotic experience. As in the other modes of borderline regression, once there is a restoration of the old objects or a substitution of new objects, the psychosis lifts. Although the psychotic episodes are seen more frequently as brief moments occurring during therapy, they can be the mode of presentation as seen in the following example:

Mrs. D. R. was a 32-year-old mother of three children who entered the day care center with a history of severe depression. During the first hours of hospitalization she appeared as a neatly dressed attractive young woman who was immediately comfortable with staff and patients. There was no objective evidence of depression. Over the weekend she overdosed with alcohol and sedatives. On Monday when she reappeared at the hospital, medications were immediately discontinued. The patient made many attempts to have her medications restored to her and refused to recognize that her inappropriate use of medication could be sufficient grounds for the discontinuance. By Monday afternoon she had become openly seductive with the resident therapist and demanded sexual relations. Her appearance and behavior had become more disorganized and bizarre. Attempts to discuss the rapid fluctuation in the patient's appearance and mental status were explained as evidence of her "illness," for which she had no understanding. When the therapist pointed out that the patient's ability to manage her own life and deal with her intense feelings seemed better prior to hospitalization, the patient became enraged and stated that she would go to another hospital where the doctors understood her better and would be less distant. She stormed out of his office and left the building.

After several minutes the therapist left his office. He returned ten minutes later and found the patient standing in a pool of blood. She had smashed the windows in his office and cut herself with the glass. Several months later she explained: "You were supposed to be in your office for me, even if I said I was leaving. I knew you would be there. When you weren't, I suddenly saw my father's face appear on the glass coming at me. A great tear appeared in his face. The world was being torn apart. I began to smash out the images."

The brief psychotic episode was followed by a second one on the same day when a meeting was held with the patient's husband. In spite of the patient's demonstrated capacity for regression, the conditions for treatment and hospitalization in terms of the patient's responsibility for her own behavior were restated. The patient began telling her husband of the doctor's callous indifference to her. When this failed to alter the stated conditions for continuing treatment in the hospital, the patient fell to the floor, began chewing on the chair leg and making bizarre moans and cries. He pulled her off and angrily stated that her behavior clearly demonstrated her need for intense treatment and her inability to be responsible for herself. The therapist maintained his position, and the patient assumed a trancelike appearance. She and her husband left the office to seek hospitalization elsewhere.

One hour later the therapist received a phone call from the patient. Her voice was clear and direct, as upon admission. She said, "Doctor, I agree." Her agreement was to continue treatment as initially stated. She was immediately discharged and seen as an outpatient for the next one and one-half years. Several brief psychotic episodes occurred during subsequent therapy sessions. Each related to real or suspected object loss. The identification of the loss in each case was followed by the lifting of the psychosis within the treatment hour. Had this patient been seen during one of her regressed states without the benefit of previous history she could easily have been diagnosed as schizophrenic.

The major clue of her actual diagnosis was the open and dramatic discussion of symptoms coupled with the mobilization of numerous people in the environment on her behalf.

The diagnosis of psychotic regression of a person with a borderline personality organization is more readily made with female patients. It is often missed in the male patients. Male borderlines are frequently diagnosed as sociopathic, simple schizophrenic, or paranoid schizophrenic personalities. The male borderline tends to show a chaotic neediness, which is marked by the presence of drug abuse (alcohol or narcotics), bisexuality as opposed to stable homosexuality, flamboyance of appearance, markedly labile effect, and self- or externally directed destructiveness. Female borderline patients tend to be more self-destructive and have less overtly antisocial behavior. The male borderline is more apt to supply his needs in a narcissistically entitled manner. In the case study that follows, the male supplied his needs in a criminal manner:

Mr. T. C. is a 19-year-old man who was admitted to the clinical research center in Lexington, Kentucky, following his third arrest for the use and sale of drugs. Prior to this period of time he had a number of admissions to local state hospitals for psychotic decompensation and criminal incarcerations for drug-related and nondrug-related crimes. After several days in the detoxification program, where he showed minimal withdrawal symptoms, he entered into an orientation group. In the midst of the group gathering he became overtly psychotic, stating that the other patients were merely actors and that people were reading his mind and really speaking of him. His distress was genuine and was immediately relieved (within minutes) by removal from the group. Several days later he returned to the group meeting and had a similar response. Staff and patients became angry with him and saw this behavior as manipulative.

With support and structure he was able to reenter the group situation and participate in the program within a few days. Once he had readjusted to the new milieu, he became involved in some of the more criminal activity and soon was asked to withdraw from the treatment program.

Subsequent follow-up revealed hospitalization at two psychiatric hospitals within the next several months followed by criminal incarceration. Evaluation in the psychiatric settings revealed intermittent marked thought disorder, delusions, and grandiosity. There was no question as to the genuineness of his psychosis. At the same time he retained a somewhat manipulative quality and continued his criminal activity. Hospitalization ended with his being discharged after some violation of hospital policies at a period when he was functioning in his premorbid fashion.

OTHER CLUES TO THE IDENTIFICATION OF THE BORDERLINE PATIENT

Multiple Disparate Diagnoses

If in reviewing hospital records or in checking with other therapists, one finds a patient has received multiple disparate diagnoses, one should suspect a borderline personality organization. Helene Deutsch[2] has described the "as-if" quality of many of these patients. These individuals have the ability to alter their mode of presentation for different observers, thus presenting various aspects of their personality to different individuals. A mistake is made in accepting the personality facet observed as being representative of the entire character structure. Otto F. Kernberg[5] has explained this in terms of the patient's use of the defense of splitting as primary to the individual's functioning.

One borderline patient carried the following diagnoses: paranoid schizophrenia, manic depressive psychosis, sociopathic personality, congenital brain damage, hyperkinesis, retardation, lesbian, alcoholic, and drug addict. All of these diagnoses, made at different times in the patient's life, were well documented. After 14 months of intensive treatment on an outpatient basis, this patient was in a stable heterosexual relationship and had moved from the freshman to senior level in college work. She had stopped all drug abuse with the one exception of occasional use of marijuana and had no further conflicts with the law.

There was little clinical evidence for any of the previous diagnoses at the end of this time.

Dramatically Altered Status

The diagnosis of borderline personality organization should be suspected when a patient enters a treatment milieu and within several hours or days has a dramatically altered status. This alteration is frequently (as noted in some of the previous examples) a shift to comfort and lack of symptomatology. Other patients who appear to be organized upon admission regress into infantile and dependent states.

Varied Staff Impressions

When different staff members in the same treatment milieu have markedly different impressions of the same patient, one should suspect that the individual in question has a borderline personality structure. A patient may be silent, irritable, and antagonistic with some staff members while intensely positive and warm with others after only a brief acquaintance. "Early conflict-laden object relations are activated prematurely in the transference in connection with the ego states that are split off from each other."[7] Good and bad, partially introjected objects are projected by the patient upon the new individuals in the environment almost immediately. Various people in the milieu are given attributes of earlier objects in the patient's life. The patient responds to these individuals not as they really are but as the earlier object in his life.

Exaggerated Requests for Care

These patients may make entitled requests for care out of proportion to their obvious needs. They seem to resent and desire the care given to more regressed individuals.

Assumption of Leadership Roles for Other Patients

Borderline patients quickly become spokesmen for other patients' anger. Within several days of admission they are the acknowledged leaders and spokespersons for the entire community and are busily organizing demands and intrigues. Frequently this involves destructive activity with other patients, such as the acquisition of drugs or the planning of escapes, liaisons, and suicides. When confronted, they explain such behavior in terms of an individual's legal or existential rights. They fail to focus upon the consequences of their behavior. In fact, they are using other patients to act out their own anger against the staff as well as their anger against the patient who may be more regressed and receiving more attention. In the role of spokesman, they may express legitimate demands of other patients. Their manner of demand and expression frequently leads the staff to become defensive and hostile. Their use of other more regressed patients provokes anger and punitive responses within the staff. These responses only support the patient's projective defenses.

A schizophrenic man was questioned about his consecutive involvement with three different female borderline patients. He stated, "They seemed to have so much energy, they are so full of life—not like me. They are able to say what I think and feel." The borderline patient's ability to dip transiently into primary process may explain the attraction that many schizophrenic patients seem to have for borderline patients. Their ability to speak of the profound emptiness and conflicts concerning human relationships are important factors in their affinity for schizophrenic patients. Borderline patients, however, are used to a rapid turnover in objects as they compulsively continue their search for the magical object that will make them better (more complete).

Frequent Urgent Problems

The borderline patient constantly presents new and urgent problems to be solved by the therapist. One gets a sense that the patient's life is a movement from one chaotic moment to another. The neophyte therapist soon learns that his attempts to solve the present problems will only involve him in a series of escalating and more disorganized issues. Should he attempt to find out the result of yesterday's crisis, he learns that the previous urgent situation is of little consequences in light of today's new and more serious difficulty.

The Quality of Creative Works

Many borderline patients invest great energy in their creative works—painting, photography, writing, and so on. Several qualities generally appear in their produtions.

Paintings in particular seemto be done in bright pastel colors. The lines tend to curve and flow together. Human figures merge and fuse. Photographs use superimposed images, shadowing, and developing techniques that give a sense of fusion and vaguely defined boundaries.

Writings are powerful and dramatic in their imagery. Oceanic feelings of engulfment, power, and merging are frequently alluded to. Issues of man's involvement in the universe and his significance are frequent themes. Personal issues are diluted with mystical philosophies and religious or social issues. There is a quality of grandiose projection and immersion.

STAFF PROBLEMS IN TREATING THE
BORDERLINE PATIENT

Since the borderline patient has difficulty relating to one individual therapist as a whole and separate object, an intensive inpatient hospitalization, with its numbers of staff, can become a smorgasbord of multiple "part objects" with whom the patient can regress and interact. Each staff person who comes into contact with the patient becomes invested with particular characteristics arising out of the patient's previous relationships and current needs. A borderline patient literally functions as if anything can be accomplished by means of finding the right person with the appropriate and omnipotent powers. Thus, each new person in the treatment setting becomes the potential person who will change the patient's life.

"We shall find that the borderline patient's belief in the physician's omnipotence corresponds to a belief in his own omnipotent powers, for he thinks that he can transform the world by means of a wish or a thought without the necessity for taking action, that is, without the need for actual work."[9] Mrs. D. R., whose case was briefly detailed previously, stated that nothing was impossible for her; it was only the matter of finding the right person or the right strategem. She was asked if she could imagine objectives that she could never achieve. With this question she became visibly agitated and replied that the thought made her feel as though she did not exist. As she began to speak of the constant use of magic and wishing in her life (e.g., walking through traffic with her eyes closed but feeling safe), she stated, "Without this belief and this power, what you are calling magic, I would be nothing; I would not exist."

The borderline patient has never seen his personal role in the development and alteration of his own life situation. Having been labeled sick, the patient considers hospitalization to be further official proof and license for complete passive dependence and the hospital to be the agent for the magical wish for fulfillment of all of his expectations.

The author has noted that men with criminal behavior who are grossly indifferent to their physical state prior to their incarceration demand all forms of medical and personal attention for the most minor ailments when in prison. These men, with severe character disorders, vehemently demanded attention for even the most insignificant conditions. It thus becomes important for the staff to remember constantly that the patient's regressed, dependent, demanding, and manipulative modes of presentation in the hospital are only one manifestation of a particular character pathology.

Even the most casual staff–patient interaction may have great implications for the patient. Psychiatric personnel commonly wish to view themselves as sensitive, warm, concerned, and benevolent individuals. There is a belief that through a warm, positive relationship the patient will learn to trust and thereby will be healed. Blanket application of such a philosophy to borderline patients can be disastrous. Frequently underlying these beliefs on the part of the staff is the wish to be the omnipotent and omniscient individual. Unless the staff member is careful, he will find himself seduced into believing that the borderline patient's immediate and intense response to him is based upon a realistic relationship. Such a belief may support one's narcissism, but it becomes a setup for the patient to maintain his pathology. The staff member, who in fact believes that he is "special" to the patient without benefit of a *previous positive relationship gained through collaborative work,* can easily be separated from the rest of the staff. He may lose his objectivity in assessing the patient's distorted view of others and his ability in helping the patient review his current situation. To be more objective might make the patient angry, and then there is the risk of losing the "special" relationship. The real risk, however, involves the staff member's losing his artificial feeling of being the warm, omnipotent healer, which is illustrated in the following case study:

Mrs. C. Y. was a 35-year-old psychiatric attendant who had worked for a number of years at the narcotics treatment center in Lexington, Kentucky. She verbally disagreed with the idea of sharing information concerning patients among the staff. She frequently stated that she had her own special and private ways of working with the men. Repeated discussions of the potential hazards of such highly individual and private work had not moved her. One morning she called the author from home stating that she did not wish to return to work because of an interaction with a patient. She met with the author and described her attempts to gain the confidence of a young addict. During the course of their intense discussions she had offered to share her lunch with this young man. Following this casual and innocent gesture, she began receiving love letters from the patient and demands that she divorce her husband and marry him. In the treatment unit he became regressed and, when Mrs. C. Y. did not appear, became withdrawn and severely depressed. Exploration with the patient revealed that the simple gesture of sharing the meal had had vast and magical meaning for him. Mrs. C. Y., when informed of this, protested that it had merely been an innocent gesture and that she could not understand how anyone could read such meaning into her behavior. She could not conceive of a perspective different from her own.

A second example gives the patient's view of the establishment of a split within the staff:

Mrs. D. M. was a 32-year-old medical technologist. She was admitted to a psychiatric service after presenting herself in an outpatient clinic and announcing that she would kill herself unless immediately hospitalized. Reluctantly, the admitting physician allowed her to enter the hospital. She immediately felt isolated and humiliated by the physician's inability to know of her distress (intuitively). On the ward she felt ignored by the staff with the exception of a night attendant who spent considerable time with her, talking to her and empathizing with her plight. Several days after admission the patient developed pharyngitis. She was enraged that the nurse would not call the harried house physician immediately. With the passing of time her anger increased because no physician appeared to relieve her distress. She described containing her rage until the night shift when the attendent was working. When he appeared on the ward, she exploded in a flurry of tossed objects. With great enthusiasm she described the sense of relief and pleasure that she experienced when the nurses were frightened by her barrage of objects. She later explained this behavior: "I knew that he [the attendant] would understand and not turn his back on me no matter what I did. He would protect me. It felt so good; I never allowed myself to do that before." The patient was in fact discharged from the hospital and complained to her therapist subsequently that the hospitalization had done no good, "I am just as suicidal." Her internal struggle with good- and bad-mother introjects had been externalized within the staff and moved no closer to resolution. Thus, the hospitalization had been of little value.

After staff members have repeatedly had their own fantasies of omnipotence and benevolence shattered by a borderline patient's rapid fluctuation in the transference, there is a tendency to turn away from (ignore) or to get into struggles with the patient and promote the patient's transfer or discharge. This sequence—that of seduction, injured staff narcissism, ignoring the patient, and increasingly destructive struggles leading to discharge or transfer—serves a defensive function to the patient and staff. The process of seduction and struggling keeps the patient engaged with objects in the environment while avoiding closer scrutiny of the patient's profound sense of emptiness.

In the struggles the patient reacts as if the staff reneged upon an agreement to fulfill *all* of his wishes. As a consequences, the patient feels entitled to and justified in any subsequent actions that he may choose to take.

Rarely are the struggling individuals able to concentrate on the fact that no such promise was ever made but that, rather, it represented a projected wish of the patient.

Another aspect of the staff–patient interaction centers about the inability of the staff to approach the patient and discuss apparent minor indiscretions on the part of the patient. As a consequence, the patient frequently escalates by exhibiting more serious and potentially destructive behavior. This forces the staff to react with exasperation rather than to take a more objective view of the patient's behavior. The patient responds to the staff anger and again fails to examine his behavior and its motivation.

A review of several situations where there were clear indications that the patient was not vested in actual treatment and the staff failed to deal with this shift in attitude revealed several common factors.

Superficially, the staff overlooked a patient's change in attitude and subsequent behavioral indiscretions because they did not want to "stir him up." The incident was too "minor," and they felt unable to refute his "reasonable explanation" that it was something "small" and "a mistake that anyone could make" or to respond to the question, "Why are you picking on me?" Other statements by the patient, such as "You expect me to change everything all at once" stymied the staff, and they failed to respond. Thus, both staff and patient agreed that only a more "serious" action should be dealt with. As expected, more destructive behavior ensued.

In retrospect, the patient is unable to extricate himself from an agreement for treatment that is no longer acceptable to him. The minor change of the agreement for treatment is the first signal for reassessment during which the therapist could help the patient verbalize the altered status. Thus, the individual could learn, less painfully, to renegotiate a plan in treatment—without the humiliation or injury of more self-destructive action. Once serious behavior has occurred there is usually little time or interest in this option.

Many times one senses a covert wish on the part of the staff to be rid of the troublesome patient. After the discharge, transfer, or the patient's leaving the hospital against advice, the staff frequently openly expresses its relief at being free of the patient. A part of the early inactivity of the staff stems from the wish to be rid of the patient.

Borderline patients openly speak of their indulgence in all forms of libidinal satisfaction. This threatens many of the staff members. Grandiose and enticing tales of drug abuse and sexual activity become threatening. The apparent misery of the patient's life is momentarily overshadowed by these exciting descriptions. Staff response becomes a group reaction formation against some of their own less conscious conflicts.

As indicated previously, effective work within an intensive-treatment setting requires the early establishment of goals, limits, expectations, and consequences of behavior on the part of both the patient and the staff. In order for this to be effective, several measures are necessary.

First of all, the staff setting new limits should not be angry, disappointed, or punitive in their dealings with the patient. The existence of these affect states within the staff will easily be noted by the patient and will be used to ignore the useful intent of the observation. Thus, a patient could easily interpret the comments of an angry staff member as, "You are only doing this because you are angry at me." Such responses on the part of the staff often represent some of their own unresolved conflicts.

Because the patient needs to learn that responses to him are the consequence of his own actions, it is useful to question a patient in the following manner: "I cannot understand why you are putting me in the position of having to reassess continuation of your stay in the hospital. Has there been some change in your own feelings about helping yourself?" Such an approach introduces the idea that the patient has a definite role in the development of his own life situation and therefore some control and autonomy.

Secondly, the staff should not view the limits and expectations as their controls over the patient. Both staff and patient must understand that the patient is not to be controlled by the staff. The overt and expressed expectations are based on the assessment of the patient's ability to function in his most compensated state. They represent a mutual agreement between the staff and the patient to become aligned with the nonregressed aspects of the patient's ego. Both parties must understand and accept that the controls rightfully reside at all times within the patient. Difficulties in the management of this responsibility can be discussed but not acted upon without consequence. The limits define the extent of the regression that the treatment unit feels that the patient needs in order to work productively and that the hospital can realistically tolerate. They become a statement of what the hospital has to offer.

Furthermore, the individual therapist and general staff must be able to respect the patient as an individual. In spite of the present regression, one must be able to maintain a more objective view based upon understanding of the character dynamics previously mentioned. The staff must understand that the patient will view the goals, limits, and expectations as punitive impositions. This will occur in spite of the patient's initial agreement and involvement in the establishment of the treatment plan. The early definition of structure in terms of a treatment plan helps to provide a consistent environment wherein the patient knows what is expected of him and what he can expect of others. For borderline patients, the experience of consistency within their environment that takes place in the hospital is unique in their lives.

SPECIFIC ROLE OF HOSPITALIZATION

Much of the previous discussion indicates some of the ways in which the hospital becomes a useful vehicle for the patient's development of a sense of autonomy and control in his previously chaotic life.

In reality, the hospital is more often just the starting point for useful therapy that must continue on an outpatient basis. Initially, the hospital functions in terms of stopping self-destructive behavior. In living with the structured treatment plan, the patient gives up the option for acting upon an impulse and thus transiently relieving his significant internal distress. When the patient gives up his option for immediate relief, depression and anxiety emerge. The patient complains about bearing such affect. This then becomes the time for the staff and therapist to discuss with the individual what are his own means to live with the burden of internal distress that he is experiencing. At such moments the patient may become angry with the staff, for they will not provide him with an immediate answer and relief:

Mrs. D. V. came to her appointment with several real crises occurring at the same time. She presented them in a chaotic, disorganized, and dramatic fashion. The therapist responded in a neutral matter-of-fact fashion, "So, what are you going to do about it?"

Mrs. D. V. said, "You're the doctor; you tell me you are supposed to help me" (by this time screaming).

Doctor, "Well, what are you going to do about it? We only have a limited time in which to try and develop an idea of how you are going to handle these circumstances."

Mrs. D. V., "I don't know. I suppose I could call a friend who might have a car." The physician wrote that down. She continued, "I could ask a neighbor." And the physician wrote that down. Mrs. D. V., "I could borrow some money from the family." Again the physician noted the patient's suggestion.

Each of these possible solutions, delivered angrily, was examined in therapy as to its relative merit. The patient reluctantly and with great irritation did, in fact, design the solution to these problems.

She returned to her next appointment with diminished anxiety and less emotional pressure. She casually mentioned that the previous problems had been solved. She did not, however, relate the relief that she felt for working out her own solutions. It was only after this process was repeated several times that she noted that relief always followed the development and carrying out of solutions of her own design.

A borderline patient always believes that words are inadequate to express and convey the distress that he is experiencing. Thus, he opts for behavioral demonstration that will express to the people around him the degree of his distress and thus bring rescue and relief. It is only by repeatedly going through the sequence noted above that the patient begins to learn that he can bear anxiety, communicate his distress, and develop solutions in a nondestructive manner that can alleviate his distress.

Because the early developmental issues in the life of a person with a borderline personality involve the inability to develop synthesized introjections of both the good and bad maternal images, the therapy with a single individual becomes useful. During the period of hospitalization, attempts should be made to channel the patient's work to a single individual who will work with the patient on a day-to-day basis focused upon the reality of the patient's situation rather than allowing the patient to indulge in the potentially explosive issues of transference.

The reality of the patient's situation will provide material from which the patient and therapist can develop an alliance of mutual positive work and concrete gains on the part of the patient. During the hospitalization the therapist should attempt to meet with the numerous individuals and agencies whom the patient has dealt with in his past. It is common for the borderline patient to have a series of friends, hospitals, physicians, and social service agencies involved in their lives. These would-be helpers are called upon in times of distress as the patient attempts to mobilize some external source of rescue. Experience has shown that many of these individuals and agencies have no knowledge of the role of the others in the patient's life. Because of this, the patient will frequently resist the idea of gathering these individuals and agencies together to share mutually their understanding of the patient's difficulties. In spite of the patient's resistance, such meetings are often productive. They clarify the roles these helping agencies might realistically play in an individual's life and provide an opportunity for the therapist to re-enforce the idea that the patient must begin to learn to function independently. The disengagement of unnecessary individuals and agencies or the limitation of their roles in an individual's life becomes useful in promoting this independence. Much of this work can be done in the context of the patient's initial, intense, and frequently positive transference to the therapist. Structuring within the hospital and within the patient's life outside of the hospital helps to bridge the gap between the inpatient experience and the patient's return to his former setting:

Miss N. D.'s current therapist was the fifth psychiatrist whom she had consulted. Her history, at age 23, included repeated episodes of violent and physically self-destructive acts. During her first session, the therapist told Miss N. D. that he would not be responsible for keeping her alive, out of the hospital, out of jail, or off of drugs. He defined his availability to her in terms of helping her deal with the problems of internal turmoil and anxiety only if she were able to contain them and bring them to the office. At no time would he become involved, as had some of her previous therapists, in obtaining her release from jail or state hospitals. (She later recounted that the therapist's initial frankness and directness of attitude had meant that she had finally found the omnipotent and controlling person whom she actually sought.)

The therapist was subsequently contacted by the patient's rehabilitation worker, local prosecutor, a police officer, and a drug counselor. With the patient's permission, the therapist spoke with them and told them that he did not support their efforts to protect the patient from the consequences of her own actions. This was followed by several self-destructive episodes, in which the patient tested the resolve of her former helpers. She was hospitalized consistently at a large state hospital. She returned to her therapist and said, "This is ridiculous. At the time I want to see you the most and work with you, I make myself unavailable."

There were no further episodes for the next year of treatment. She explained, "I always felt safe when I did things. They would protect me." The availability of her previous helpers for rescue in effect promoted self-destructive behavior.

LENGTH OF HOSPITALIZATION

In most instances a brief hospitalization tends to obviate the patient's potential for regression. Because of the numbers of staff and the difficulties in communication within the intensive treatment setting, the longer a hospitalization, the greater the chance for splitting within the staff and destructive regression on the part of the patient. The author's experiences have shown that a one-week to two-week hospitalization, in the context of the structure noted earlier, seems to be optimal for most people who have a borderline personality. Beyond that time regression seems inevitable. In two instances the author has reviewed hospitalization periods of six to seven months. The individuals involved progressively relinquished all sense of responsibility for their own behavior and ultimately were sent to state hospitals where, within a period of 7 to 10 days, they had reconstituted themselves and were discharged from the hospitals completely. They then resumed living and caring for themselves in an out-of-the hospital environment.

After a brief hospitalization in which there has been an attempt to structure the process of therapy with the patient, periodic rehospitalization may be required when the individual is in danger of serious self-destructive behavior. If the pattern develops in which the patient repeatedly avoids resolving a situation by arranging readmission, one should consider hospitalization at large custodial state hospitals and an interruption of treatment until the patient is once again able to assume responsibility for his own existence.

Although most borderline patients require only a brief initial hospitalization there seems to be a small subgroup who do require prolonged inpatient hospitalization. These individuals seem to be able to maintain ego splits of such proportion that they are unable to view in any useful manner their regressive and self-destructive impulses unless they are blatantly demonstrated:

Mrs. J. K. is a 35-year-old college instructor with a high degree of competence in her work. Prior to admission she made two serious suicide attempts. From the first hour of admission to the hospital she appeared comfortable and busied herself helping other patients and staff. She demonstrated no signs of her previously noted depression. The evident precipitant of her suicide attempts appeared to be the end of a relationship of six years' duration. Several times during her admission she made serious attempts to kill herself. These attempts were carried out with great determination and were followed by brief periods (up to a half-hour in length) in which the patient was rigid and uncommunicative, although apparently aware of all within the environment. These episodes ended abruptly and the patient was lucid and communicative. She could factually describe some of her feelings prior to the moment of the suicide attempt. For the patient, there seemed to be no affective or cognitive tie between the rational discussion following these attempts and the behavior during them. The staff was seriously frightened by the patient and demanded that she immediately be transferred to a more closed environment. After several days during which the patient had functioned in her usual competent style, the staff altered its position and requested the chief resident that she be kept within the hospital. The staff denied their previous anxiety and could not view the unchanged clinical status of the patient as presenting serious potential danger. The patient was in fact transferred to another intensive treatment center that provided a locked setting. Her pattern of competence continued and was marked by periodic serious suicide attempts. Because of the rigid isolation of affect and thought with regard to these impulsive attempts, there seemed to be no brief means of bridging the gap between the split ego states. A longer hospitalization seemed to offer the only hope for connecting these separate states.

CONCLUSION

Borderline patients—some of whom are labeled sociopathic personalities, pseudoneurotic schizophrenia, schizoid personalities, primitive-oral hysterics, and so forth—present major treatment problems for inpatient treatment settings. The patients have the capacity to make rapid progressive or regressive changes, form intense relationships, appear comfortable through the massive use of projection and denial, and easily touch unconscious conflicts within the individual staff members. These abilities seem to be the source of the staff's bewilderment, panic, resignation, and anger when dealing with such patients. Early diagnosis can help orient the staff to meet effectively the patients' needs without a regression on both parts.

Hospitalization is initially used to interrupt the current pathologic occurrence. This can be followed by an attempt to help the borderline patient deal with his life situation in less destructive ways. Because the patient's character pathology manifests in a range of interactions, close attention to activity in the ward milieu will reveal the repetition of the patient's usual mode of interaction. Scrutiny and clarification of the behavior can assist the patient in beginning to view his behavior as a process of decision and choice rather than as a mere reaction to external circumstances (victim of circumstance). For this initial phase of therapy to be effective the staff must be consistent in their individual and combined dealings with the patient. A failure of one or more staff members to deal with the patient in the agreed manner can become the nidus for splitting and regression on the part of the patient.

As noted earlier, when the patient gives up the option for destructive action in the search of transient relief or comfort, he is agreeing to try not only to bear but also to deal with a profound state of depression. Tolerance for this previously avoided state is gained through steady realistic gains in therapy and the establishment of a predictable environment upon which the patient can depend. At first this is a concrete process, as when the therapist in the example given carefully wrote down all the patient's suggestions for solving her problem or when the hospital staff literally defines expectations and limits. Later, after a period of consistent experience that has led the patient to learn that it is possible to anticipate realistically the responses of people and to plan one's decisions constructively, the work moves to the more painful area of uncovering and resolving earlier conflicts.

In the early concrete phase of therapy the patient learns by testing the agreements and resolve of his therapeutic mentors. Anticipating this, the staff working with such an individual should be wary of excess involvement in the success or failure of the patient in any particular endeavor. It is more useful to remain the steady observer who helps the patient review the options of his situation, the consequences, the general predictability of outcome and the usual uncertainty that anyone must live with. Excess involvement of the staff in any single growth step can lead to disappointment and withdrawal from the patient if it fails, or it can lead to overresponsiveness, which makes the patient wary as to whether the change is for him or for his helper.

In a hospital that is prepared to meet the needs of borderline patients a hospitalization period of one or two weeks is usually adequate to bring the patient to the point of a stable, tolerable depression. The subsequent process of therapy can generally be conducted on an outpatient basis. Occasional crises may require brief hospitalization.

REFERENCES

1. Adler G: Hospital treatment of borderline patients. Am J Psychiatry 130:32–76, 1973
2. Deutsch H: Some forms of emotional disturbance and their relationships to schizophrenia. Int J Psychoanal 44:282–292, 1963
3. Freidman HJ: Some problems of in-patient management with borderline patients. Am J Psychiatry 126:47–52, 1969

4. Frosch J: The psychotic character: Clinical psychiatric considerations. Psychiat Q 38:81–96, 1964
5. Kernberg OF: Structural derivatives of object relationships. Int J Psychoanal 47:236–253, 1966
6. Kernberg OF: A psychoanalytic classification of character pathology. J Am Psychoanal Assoc 18:800–822, 1970
7. Knight RP: Borderline states, in Knight RP, Friedman CR (eds): Psychoanalytic Psychiatry and Psychology, vol I. New York, International Universities Press, 1962, pp 97–109
8. Modell AH: Primitive object relationships and predisposition to schizophrenia. Int J Psychoanal 44:282–292, 1963
9. Murray JM: Narcissism and the ego ideal. Paper presented at the Boston Psychoanalytic Society and Institute, March 27, 1963

Daniel H. Jacobs

4

The Borderline or Psychotic Character in the Prison Setting

Individuals with antisocial personalities or who engage in criminal acts are rarely diagnosed as "borderline" when seen in the court room or in community settings. Rather, the term seems to be reserved currently for persons who have no predominant pattern of deviance, addiction, or antisocial action, despite the fact that Wilhelm Reich, Edward Glover, Melitta Schmideberg, and others considered such cases originally as borderline states. In current discussions elements of ego disorganization and regression appear to be necessary in making the diagnosis of "borderline."

As long as tension can be discharged and conflict avoided through drug taking, alcoholism, or delinquency, many individuals can maintain stable character patterns and avoid ego regression. In the isolated prison setting, however, these familiar patterns of adaptation are denied to the inmate, and, as Daniel H. Jacobs discusses in his chapter, transient decompensation may occur. Disturbances of reality sense, overwhelming feelings of anxiety, self-destructive behavior, and other symptomatology or behavioral manifestations then occur that are indistinguishable from the picture of the psychotic character of John Frosch or borderline states as described by Robert P. Knight and other writers. Jacobs emphasizes the importance for the prison staff of recognizing and understanding such regressive phenomena and of handling them appropriately.

In prison, men who by their behavior and history had been thought to have a relatively fixed character disorder in which sociopathic features were prominent often begin to exhibit more serious signs of ego disorganization—signs usually associated with the "borderline" or psychotic character. Imprisonment presents particular stresses. On unfamiliar

63

ground, without family or friends, his fate in the hands of strangers, the prisoner struggles for some sense of mastery, both over his surroundings and over his feelings. New alliances are made in prison; new rules must be obeyed. Feelings of extreme helplessness in the face of an arbitrary and often hostile authority must be dealt with if personal integrity and identity are to be maintained. The anomie of the prison setting undermines the individual's sense of himself.

For some men the stress of confinement, coupled with the interference with their established behavior patterns, produces a marked change in their ability to maintain psychological equilibrium. In most prisons, the capacity for immediate discharge of impulse, for physical escape or for flight through alcohol, drugs, sexual activity, or antisocial behavior is limited if not entirely absent. As the pressure to maintain identity increases and usual methods of defending against feelings of dissolution are limited, symptoms usually associated with borderline states become apparent. What then seems like a sudden shift in the prisoner's behavior often leads to confusion and misunderstanding on the part of prison authorities. In this chapter, the type of regressive behavior most often seen, the type of confusion it creates, and the possible consequences of such confusion will be briefly explored.

Anyone working in a prison for any length of time has observed some prisoner shaken by severe anxiety or other strong affect in whom there is a significant loss of reality testing. These symptoms, often of limited duration, are precipitated by a change in the prisoner's relationship to the prison or to those important to him outside its walls. When the symptoms are acute, the prisoner will often request medication as a way of dealing with painful affects and feelings of dissolution. These regressive, psychoticlike states take a variety of forms.

There may be, for instance, an increased inability to separate clearly waking and dreaming states—a type of confusion often associated with borderlines.

In Case I, a 23-year-old black prisoner with a long history of car thefts and larceny complained of increased anxiety accompanied by insomnia and fatigue of several days' duration. He initially requested tranquilizers and medication for sleep. He had experienced frequent insomnia at home with occasional nightmares. He denied, however, difficulties in distinguishing between dreams and reality in the past. He now told of an incident in which a hooded and robed figure with a dog had stood by his bed at night in the prison dormitory. Although he knew there were no dogs in the prison and that a hooded figure was unlikely to have appeared, he could not with certainty deny that the event had taken place. Only after several sessions with a therapist was he able to conclude that the event must have been a dream related to his anxiety about moving into both a new job and a new dormitory in the prison.[1]

Another regressive pattern frequently seen is a marked increase in somatic symptoms accompanied by a transient delusional belief on the part of the prisoner that he is ill, despite repeated examinations and reassurances to the contrary. Such symptoms frequently occur in men who have rarely been ill outside of prison and who showed little interest in routine medical care prior to incarceration. Any attempt to indicate to the inmate that his problem is not physical may be met with denial and verbal abuse. Such increase in somatic concerns is often seen in the course of therapy, but it is by no means confined to the psychiatric patient population of the prison. An example of such concerns accompanied by a temporary loss in reality testing is seen in Case II:

A 35-year-old divorced father of five, a chronic alcoholic, was serving four to eight years in a state prison for armed robbery. While in prison, he was seen in weekly psychotherapy. He had no history of previous hypochondriasis. During treatment, however, he began to demand from the psychiatrist large quantities of medication for severe headaches. When refused, he became annoyed. Shortly after this refusal, the patient began to speak of his childhood, his feelings of rejection by his father, and his suspicions that he was not, after all, his father's child. At this point, feeling both a lack of nurturance by his father and by the therapist, he began to complain about severe pain in his teeth. He visited the prison dentist, convinced that his teeth were rotting, and that the only way to rid himself of his pain was a full-mouth extraction. When the dentist refused, the patient became enraged, refusing to appear either for further dental or psychotherapy sessions. He was, after a while, able to return to treatment, give up the somatic delusion, and begin to understand its relation to his feelings of rejection, aggression, and self-punishment.

Still other types of regressive behavior are noted when men are placed in isolation either as punishment or for protection. Alone in a cell without the varied sensory input and motor activity so necessary to support his shaky sense of himself, the prisoner may be overwhelmed by feelings of dissolution. Frightened, he then makes frantic attempts at resolution. There may be an increase in violence, suicide attempts, and self-mutilative behavior. Wrist cutting, arm slashing, and the swallowing of glass or razor blades is not uncommon for prisoners in isolation. Such acts may be accompanied by an altered state of consciousness in which feelings of derealization and depersonalization are present. The acts often are designed consciously or unconsciously to get attention and thus increase interaction and sensory input. Examples of such primitive defenses against separation and subsequent feelings of dissolution can be seen in Case III:

A 26-year-old white southerner convicted of armed robbery was placed in isolation because of threatening to hurt a fellow inmate. The patient and his family had a long history of violence, robberies, and gun battles. He appeared generally angry, distrustful, and unrepentent. Although he had been in a variety of detention centers and jails since adolescence, he had no previous history of psychiatric treatment. He appeared impulsive and unruly, but never psychotic. In isolation he initially tore up bedding and ripped out the plumbing. When interviewed, he gave no explanation other than wanting to get out of isolation. Although he appeared markedly anxious, he denied any feelings other than anger with the authorities. When not released, he cut his wrists in several places. When finally placed in the prison hospital, he became frightened of leaving and began to express fears of dying. For several days he lay in a semistuporous state. His symptoms subsided as the precipitants for the threatening behavior that led to his being placed in isolation were explored. He had been surprised when his wife had not worn her wedding ring on her most recent visit to him. He felt she might be seeing another man and would soon divorce him. He was, however, unable to tell her of his concerns. The next day, he temporarily mastered his sense of helplessness and gave vent to his rage by bullying another inmate. This behavior only led to his being placed in isolation, where heightened fears of separation and death were handled in an increasingly regressive manner. When his relationship with his wife was explored and alternative ways of dealing with his distress discussed, the patient was able to leave the hospital.

Such severe, even if temporary, alterations in ego functioning are often regarded by prison personnel, including physicians, as essentially dishonest. They consider these actions conscious, manipulative attempts at gratification. To the prison personnel they are just another game from the sociopath's large bag of tricks. Such impressions are reinforced if the symptoms disappear rapidly once gratification is achieved, whether it be the medication requested, release from isolation, or change in a living or job situation.

The view of such symptomotology as manipulative is not, of course, without merit. There is often a clear secondary gain in such behavior. There is, too, the accompanying and constant fear upon the part of staff members, whether professional or not, of being made a fool of by the convict. It is not easy to distinguish between a genuine and serious alteration in defensive structure and malingering. To take seriously all such regressive behavior and to grant the inmate's requests may expose the staff member to accusations of being "soft" by both inmates and other personnel. Since psychiatric evaluation is often unavailable or not desired by the inmate, the prison staff is left in the dilemma either of granting what appears an unreasonable request and feeling manipulated or of denying the request and facing the irrational anger and abuse of the prisoner in his repeated and persistent attempts to get what he feels he needs.

The staff's own anger with the situation may manifest itself in an incomplete or incorrect evaluation of ego function. Behind such incomplete understanding often lies the desire to be rid of a troublesome patient. Indeed, such wishes may be realized. If the inmate's behavior is seen only as manipulative and if suicide gestures, aggressive outbursts, or severe hypochondriasis continue, the chances of the inmate's being transferred to some other institution are substantially increased.

While prison staff are quick to recognize the secondary gain in such psychoticlike behavior, they often do not appreciate the severity of the underlying illness. This is due, in part, to the failure in most prisons to provide staff with even the most rudimentary concepts of ego psychology and psychodynamics so that they can make a more meaningful assessment of behavior. Marguerite Q. Warren has pointed out that much of the literature in the field of corrections is still written as if all offenders were alike.[9] Investigators, such as M. Q. Warren, D. Hunt, and O. Harvey, are currently working on typologies of offenders utilizing primarily ego psychology concepts in which state of ego integration, level of psychosocial development, complexity of perceptual differentiation, and the like would be evaluated.[4,5] To date, however, there is very little understanding that rehabilitative techniques most appropriate to the task of strengthening the coping powers of the inmates must be prescribed by the very nature of the ego structure and the state of ego development.[2]

There is still a tendency to label criminals as character disorders or sociopaths without the more careful analysis of character pathology that Otto F. Kernberg, for example, has outlined.[6,7,8] More rigorous analysis might reveal that when the usual impulsive and antisocial behavior is limited, the borderline or psychotic character structure of many inmates becomes readily apparent. John Frosch has observed that

> the psychotic character bears the same relationship to psychotic symptoms as the neurotic character does to neurotic symptoms. Under certain circumstances, stresses and strains ... decompensation or regressive adaptations may take place and psychotic symptoms and features may become manifest, just as neurotic symptoms become manifest under similar circumstances in the neurotic character.[3]

These considerations may have practical benefits in a prison setting, where careful diagnosis and understanding of behavior, if only for security reasons, is essential. To consider bizarre behavior or unusual demandingness as only manipulative is incomplete and dangerous. Such inadequate understanding and the accompanying failure to appreciate the regressive capacity in the inmate may have serious consequences in terms of suicide or of harm to others.

By trying to uncover the exact nature of the stress upon the prisoner and by evaluating the ego's capacity to deal with that particular stress, tragic consequences may be avoided. A seemingly slight stress may precipitate overwhelming feelings of helplessness and dissolution, which are made even harder to handle by the limitations on expression and action that imprisonment imposes. If the prison staff understands that the inmate is trying to cope with these feelings through increased demands, distortion of reality testing, or other overtly psychotic symptoms, they can initially try to support the weakened ego through a number of therapeutic measures designed to alleviate the difficulty. Brief psychotherapy, medication, job or living change, removal from isolation, or an increase in sensory input while the inmate remains isolated are some of the immediately available measures.

The way in which a man responds to the difficulties of prison life and the methods of coping that he employs can reveal his psychopathology and the help he needs. The psychotic character structure that often underlies antisocial behavior may become more readily apparent. Understanding the meaning of an inmate's psychoticlike behavior amidst his anger, insults, and distrust and responding to it accurately can often be the first steps in the development of a therapeutic relationship that might not otherwise have been begun.

REFERENCES

1. Blum J: Personal communication
2. Freeman H, Hildebrand C, Ayre D: A classification system that prescribes treatment. Social Casework 46:423–429, 1965
3. Frosch: Psychoanalytic considerations of the psychotic character. Psychoanal Assoc 18:24–50, 1970
4. Harvey O, Hunt D, Schroder H: Conceptual Systems and Personality Organization. New York, John Wiley, 1961
5. Hunt D, Hardt R: Developmental stage, delinquency and differential treatment. J Research in Crime and Delinquency 2:20–31, 1965
6. Kernberg OF: Borderline personality organization. Am Psychoanal Assoc 15:641–685, 1967
7. Kernberg OF: The treatment of patients with borderline personality organization. Int J Psychoanal 49:600–619, 1968
8. Kernberg OF: A psychoanalytic classification of character pathology. J Am Psychoanal Assoc 18:800–822, 1970
9. Warren Q: Classification of offenders as an aid to efficient management and effective treatment. J Criminal Law, Criminology and Police Science 62:239–268, 1971

Samuel B. Guze

5

Differential Diagnosis of the
Borderline Personality Syndrome

One wonders if there ever has been in psychiatry a syndrome about which so much has been written while so little agreement has existed in regard to its phenomenology. Samuel B. Guze points to the great range of clinical features that have been included in discussions of borderline cases without adequate data regarding the frequency with which these manifestations occur either by themselves or in combination with other clinical features—the hallmark of a verifiable syndrome. Without the establishment of a consistent grouping of such clinical features it is difficult for meaningful research to proceed.

Guze argues that the establishment of a diagnostic entity in psychiatry, as in other clinical fields, requires consistent data on the natural history of the disorder and its delimitation from other conditions. These criteria, he believes, have not been fulfilled in the case of the "borderline syndrome." The borderline's borders with sociopathy, alcoholism, drug dependence, schizophrenia, and hysterical and affective disorders have not, according to Guze, been established.

Before the differential diagnosis of the borderline syndrome can be discussed usefully, the condition must be defined well enough to make clear which patients are being included. Unfortunately, thus far the disorder has been described so vaguely that any differential diagnosis must of necessity involve a wide range of psychiatric disorders. Publications reveal definitions so general and abstract that it is hard to be sure that the

This work was supported in part by the following grant: AA-00209, HEW, ADAMHA, 1 June 1972 through 31 May 1975.

authors are all referring to the same kinds of patients. The following are representative quotations:

> The clinical picture of the borderline ranges on a spectrum from those who live constantly teetering precariously on the verge of psychosis with frequent forays into decompensatory pictures characterizing their course of life, to those in whom the psychotic-like features may be well masked by a rigid adaptation only to appear during periods of decompensation under severe stress and in unstructured situations.[3]

> I am thus proposing that the diagnosis of the borderline patient involves a distinction between problems determined by unresolved intrapsychic conflict, regressive changes attributable to a period of serious developmental or situational stress, and finally, significant failure to establish certain basic ego functions.[7]

> Such issues as the state of the borderline patient's ego, his capacity to tolerate depression or anxiety, the characteristic defensive structure, the quality of object relations, their narcissistic intensity, the role of guilt, the quality and quantity of the anger, as well as the presence of possible modifying positive affect need to be considered before we can claim to have adequately defined a clinical picture of patients in this group.[2]

Otto F. Kernberg, in a detailed theoretical discussion, presents the following as a basis for the "presumptive" diagnosis of the borderline personality:

> Patients suffering from borderline personality organization present themselves with what superficially appear to be typical neurotic symptoms. However, the neurotic symptoms and character pathology of these patients have peculiarities which point to an underlying borderline personality organization. Only a careful diagnostic examination will reveal the particular combinations of different neurotic symptoms. No symptoms are pathognomonic, but the presence of two, and especially of three, symptoms among those which will be enumerated strongly points to the possibility of an underlying borderline personality organization. All of these descriptive elements are only presumptive diagnostic signs of borderline personality organization. The definite diagnosis depends on characteristic ego pathology and not on the descriptive symptoms.[5]

Kernberg then goes on to list the following "symptomatic categories"—but cautions that it is "not an exhaustive list": anxiety, polysymptomatic neurosis, polymorphous perverse sexual trends, the "classical" prepsychotic personality structures, impulse neurosis and addictions, and "lower level" character disorders.

Kernberg provides additional comments for each of the symptomatic categories to clarify his meaning. Under anxiety he notes, "Such patients tend to present chronic, diffuse, free-floating anxiety. This symptom becomes particularly meaningful when a variety of other symptoms or pathological character traits are present." Polysymptomatic neurosis includes "multiple phobias . . . obsessive compulsive symptoms which have acquired secondary ego syntonicity . . . multiple, elaborate, or bizarre conversion symptoms, especially if they are chronic, or even a monosymptomatic conversion reaction of a severe kind extending over many years' duration . . . dissociative reactions, especially hysterical 'twilight states' and fugues, and amnesia accompanied by disturbances of consciousness . . . hypochondriasis . . . and paranoid and hypochondriacal trends with any other symptomatic neurosis." The polymorphous perverse sexual trends include "heterosexual and homosexual promiscuity with sadistic elements" and "patients whose manifest sexual behavior is completely inhibited but whose conscious fantasies, and especially masturbatory fantasies, involve multiple perverse trends as necessary conditions for achieving sexual gratification." Under the prepsychotic personality structures Kernberg lists "paranoid personality," "schizoid personality," and "hypomanic personality and the 'cyclothymic' personality organization with strong hypomanic trends." Impulse neurosis and addictions include "alcoholism, drug addictions, certain forms of psychogenic obesity, and kleptomania. . . . This group also merges with the 'acting-out' personality disorders in general. . . ." As "lower level" character disorders Kernberg includes "severe character pathology typically represented by the chaotic and impulse-ridden character. . . ." He concludes, "All clearcut antisocial personality structures that I have examined have presented a typical borderline personality organization."[5]

It should be clear from these definitions and descriptions that a wide range of patients are included in the category of borderline personality. This diagnostic confusion stems from the absence of *systematic clinical* data about the patients described. Most reports are limited to the presentation of a few patients; others give only the most general criteria. A major attempt at systematic study of borderline personality explicitly decided *against* a structured psychiatric interview in favor of an unstructured one.[4]

Thus, there is little systematic information concerning the presence or absence of a wide array of psychiatric symptoms that might help delimit the disorder and make differential diagnosis more focused and effective. Drinking problems, drug abuse, temper outbursts, delinquency, conversion symptoms, sexual disturbances, and suicide attempts are noted in many of the case reports, but nowhere are data given concerning the frequency of such problems in the entire sample; in fact, it appears likely that questions dealing with these symptoms were not asked of all patients.

The essential elements in the recognition and definition of a valid clinical psychiatric syndrome have been described by Eli Robins and Samuel B. Guze under "five phases."

1. Clinical Description. In general, the first step is to describe the clinical picture of the disorder. This may be a single striking clinical feature or a combination of clinical features thought to be associated with one another. Race, sex, age at onset, precipitating factors, and other items may be used to define the clinical picture more precisely. The clinical picture thus does not include only symptoms.

2. Laboratory Studies. Included among laboratory studies are chemical, physiological, radiological, and anatomical (biopsy and autopsy) findings. Certain psychological tests, when shown to be reliable and reproducible, may also be considered laboratory studies in this context. Laboratory findings are generally more reliable, precise, and reproducible than are clinical descriptions. When consistent with a defined clinical picture, they permit a more refined classification. Without such a defined clinical picture, their value may be considerably reduced. Unfortunately, consistent and reliable laboratory findings have not yet been demonstrated in the more common psychiatric disorders.

3. Delimitation from Other Disorders. Since similar clinical features and laboratory findings may be seen in patients suffering from different disorders (e.g., cough and blood in the sputum in lobar pneumonia, bronchiectasis, and bronchogenic carcinoma), it is necessary to specify exclusion criteria so that patients with other illnesses are not included in the group to be studied. These criteria should also permit exclusion of borderline cases and doubtful cases (an undiagnosed group) so that the index group may be as homogeneous as possible.

4. Follow-Up Study. The purpose of the follow-up study is to determine whether or not the original patients are suffering from some other defined disorder that could account for the original clinical picture. If they are suffering from another such illness, this finding suggests that the original patients did not comprise a homogeneous group and that it is necessary to modify the diagnostic criteria. In the absence of known etiology or pathogenesis, which is true of the more common psychiatric disorders, marked differences in out-

come, such as between complete recovery and chronic illness, suggest that the group is not homogeneous. This latter point is not as compelling in suggesting diagnostic heterogeneity as is the finding of a change in diagnosis. The same illness may have a variable prognosis, but until we know more about the fundamental nature of the common psychiatric illnesses, marked differences in outcome should be regarded as a challenge to the validity of the original diagnosis.

5. Family Study. Most psychiatric illnesses have been shown to run in families, whether [or not] the investigations were designed to study hereditary or environmental causes. Independent of the question of etiology, therefore, the finding of an increased prevalence of the same disorder among the close relatives of the original patients strongly indicates that one is dealing with a valid entity.

We hope it is apparent that these five phases interact with one another so that new findings in any one of the phases may lead to modifications in one or more of the other phases. The entire process is therefore one of continuing self-rectification and increasing refinement leading to more homogeneous diagnostic grouping. Such homogeneous diagnostic grouping provides the soundest base for studies of etiology, pathogenesis, and treatment. The role of heredity, family interactions, intelligence, education, and sociological factors are most simply, directly, and reliably studied when the group studied is as homogeneous as possible.[6]

To describe a syndrome effectively and delimit it from other similar conditions, a search for the characteristic features of the other conditions must be carried out. This can only mean a systematic and at least partially structured interview.

Systematic observations in the hospital of interactions with staff and other patients and standardized psychological tests, while desirable, are not substitutes for systematic clinical histories. Valid psychiatric diagnoses, i.e., diagnoses that predict course, prognosis, and familial patterns of psychopathology, require longitudinal clinical histories that include age of the patient, mode of onset of the illness, description of the symptoms that make up the illness, data concerning previous course including remissions and exacerbations, past history of medical and psychiatric difficulties, a family history of psychiatric disorders, and a comprehensive social history.

In the absence of published data concerning these items it is impossible to estimate how many of the patients described as borderline might fulfill the criteria for sociopathy, alcoholism, drug dependence, hysteria, primary or secondary affective disorders, or schizophreniform illness.[1] Each of these diagnoses might be appropriate for some of the borderline patients.

If the borderline syndrome is meant to include all of these disorders, its usefulness as a diagnosis is limited because it cannot be used for predicting course, complications, response to treatment, and other important features. The latter will vary depending upon whether the patient's illness conforms to one of the above disorders or another.

If the borderline syndrome is meant as an additional diagnosis, based upon certain features that are more "fundamental" than the clinical features used to diagnose hysteria, alcoholism, and so forth, evidence needs to be provided that the basic features are, in fact, independent of the clinical criteria. Thus, borderline patients must be described with and without the features of hysteria, with and without the features of sociopathy, and so on. Further, borderline patients must be similarly compared to patients with affective disorders, schizophrenia, and other conditions usually excluded in reports of the syndrome.

In conclusion, it must be stressed again that the differential diagnosis of the borderline syndrome includes a wide range of psychiatric disorders because, thus far, the syndrome has been described so generally that patients who are probably suffering from alcoholism, drug dependence, hysteria, sociopathy, schizophreniform conditions, and affective illnesses are included. Systematic clinical studies—based at least in part on structured interviews, follow-up, and examination of close relatives—are needed before the validity of the syndrome can be established.

REFERENCES

1. Feighner JP, Robins E, Guze SB, et al: Diagnostic criteria for use in psychiatric research. Arch Gen Psychiat 26:57–63, 1972
2. Friedman HJ: Letters to the editor. Am J Psychiatry 126:1677, 1970
3. Frosch J: Technique in regard to some specific ego defects in treatment of borderline patients. Psychiatr Q 45:216, 1971
4. Grinker RR Sr, Werble B, Drye RC: The Borderline Syndrome. New York, Basic Books, 1968
5. Kernberg O: Borderline personality organization. J Am Psychoanal Assoc 15:641–685, 1967
6. Robins E, Guze SB: Establishment of diagnostic validity in psychiatric illness: Its application to schizophrenia. Am J Psychiatry 126:983–987, 1970
7. Zetzel ER: A developmental approach to the borderline patient. Am J Psychiatry 127:867–871, 1971

Donald F. Klein

6

Psychopharmacology and the Borderline Patient

Donald F. Klein has for several years been interested in using the response to psychopharmacological agents for differential diagnosis, especially among the character and behavior disorders. Like Samuel B. Guze, Klein feels that the case for establishing the specific diagnosis of a borderline syndrome has not been established on the basis of a predictable response to psycho-active drugs or on the basis of any other recognized criteria. Klein notes that Roy R. Grinker and his co-workers have included four groups within the "borderline syndrome" that are really quite distinct from one another. He observes that these groups resemble clinically other groups of patients (not labeled borderline) who have been differentiated on the basis of their response to particular types of medication. Group II, for example—patients demonstrating certain forms of emotional instability and affective lability—resemble patients who have been found to respond well to phenothiazine drugs and to lithium.

Klein questions the diagnostic usefulness of the structural approach or the emphasis in psychoanalysis upon drives. He argues that affects lend themselves better than do these more abstract notions to the verification of the response to drugs or other forms of treatment and are, therefore, of greater diagnostic and prognostic value. Affects are "targetable," and clinical changes related to improvement in emotional states can be readily ascertained.

*This chapter was benefited by the careful reviews of Rachel Gittelman-Klein, Ph.D., and Alfreda Howard, M. A.

Klein's interest in the diagnostic use of drugs has led him to emphasize the importance of a longitudinal approach, or dimension, in the differentiation of psychiatric syndromes. A sequence of examinations over time (what Klein calls "modal sequential drug treatment patterns") are of greater value than examinations at a single point in time or "before-and-after" observations. Research that applies these approaches to borderline conditions is virtually impossible at the present time because of the failure to differentiate consistent, discrete affective, or other phenomenological characteristics in these conditions.

DIAGNOSTIC CONSIDERATIONS

The term "borderline states" has developed unfortunately into a device for obscuring (from ourselves and others) uncertainties about the phenomenology, pathophysiology, and course of certain patients. Some patients simply do not clearly fit any of the currently available diagnostic stereotypes. Others do conform to a diagnostic pattern, but the correspondence is not perceived. In particular, a patient may qualitatively belong to a diagnostic class that implies mild severity (e.g., phobic neurosis), but the severity of symptomatology or life disruption is such that the diagnostician prefers a label with more malignant implications.

To complicate matters further, many patients express themselves in an imaginative or metaphorical fashion during emotional crises, making it difficult for the examiner to question them closely or to elicit cooperation. A statement intended by the patient to have an "as-if" quality may easily be misinterpreted as a statement of a delusion or hallucination, e.g., "I'm nothing. I've disappeared." Patients who have undergone extended analytically oriented psychotherapy are particularly prone to express themselves in "deep primary process" terminology that can lead the clinician to presume a weak ego rather than a linguistic facade. Also, hysterical and malingering patients may purposely mislead the examiner. Such interactions obscure the diagnostic data by blurring the patterns.

Yet another difficulty is part of the diagnostician's unenviable lot; he is confronted not only by the patient's complexities, but also by the interactive realities of his own implicit and explicit peer relationships as they affect both his self-esteem and impression management.

Game theory helps us see that psychiatrists and psychologists endanger their self-esteem and reputation by making a diagnosis that can be proved wrong. Diagnoses that cannot be proven wrong are certainly preferable. Therefore, in an uncertain world, the safest procedure is to diagnose a potential or "borderline" psychosis even in the absence of psychotic manifestations. The reasoning is simple. A patient who is diagnosed as a potential psychotic either manifests psychosis, proving the keen ability of the diagnostician, or no psychotic manifestations ever come to light. When the latter occurs, there is no "real" error; it is simple testimony to the diagnostician's ability to see past the obvious, and/or to his superior therapeutic abilities that have prevented the development of manifest psychosis. Therefore, the diagnosis of potential psychosis, i.e., borderline state, always has honorific results.

On the other hand, a diagnosis of neurosis, character disorder, and so forth, is open to both internal reproach as well as public contradiction and subsequent obloquy if the patient becomes psychotic. Worse, even if the patient remains manifestly nonpsychotic, the diagnosis is open to verbal contradiction by other clinicians, who then have the self-ascribed, one-up status of superior perceptual depth. Therefore, making such a diagnosis is always asking for trouble. Since we strive for security, satisfaction, and self-esteem (at least), it is not surprising that the diagnosis of borderline state, latent schizophrenia, and the like, is made remarkably often. A further value to such diagnoses is that they preserve intact the pristine belief that intensive psychotherapy is the uniformly effective treatment of choice for neurosis since failures will only occur with the pseudoneurotic patient.

SCHIZOPHRENIA AND PSEUDONEUROTIC SCHIZOPHRENIA

Schizophrenia is a psychiatric concept that has led to widespread confusion. The original definition by Emil Kraepelin of "dementia praecox" (defined as identical with schizophrenia by the American Psychiatric Association Diagnostic Manual) was based upon course of illness. The term "dementia praecox" distinguished deteriorating patients from other psychotics, such as manic-depressives, who did not deteriorate although they might relapse. In order to make a rational prognosis, Kraepelin isolated certain distinguishing initial clinical features of deteriorated patients and used these to define a syndrome with a specific poor prognosis. These traits were all clearly of psychotic quality and intensity.

Eugen Bleuler, on the other hand, was less impressed with the predictive utility of such psychotic symptomatology. Rather, he emphasized other clinical features, such as autism and ambivalence, that were assumed to identify a disorder of association (splitting) considered by him to be the basis of the schizophrenic process. These traits were believed to be discernible even during nonpsychotic periods. These characteristics were not segregated for their prognostic import and indeed did not identify a disorder that necessarily progressed to deterioration. For this reason, even if one were able to apply Bleuler's ill-defined criteria systematically and identify this fundamental psychological defect, thereby diagnosing schizophrenia, one would still be left without any prognostic ability.

This trend to segregate patients on the basis of some inferred psychopathological process and to divorce this categorization from the practical utility of prediction received further emphasis in the labels "pseudoneurotic" or "pseudopsychopathic" schizophrenia or borderline state. Patients so labeled need not manifest examinational signs of either Kraepelinian-defined or Bleulerian-defined schizophrenia. The reasons for the assumption of a continuum between these states and the classically defined schizophrenia are not clear. It is meritorious to make the creative effort necessary to describe a syndrome, but it is unwise for the psychiatric community to accept such syndromes uncritically, without clinical and statistical documentation.

Paul H. Hoch and Phillip Polatin,[3] who developed the concept of pseudoneurotic schizophrenia, have stated that some diagnosticians consider these cases to be psychoneurotic, but since these patients are refractory to exploratory psychotherapy, they argue that there must be a basic difference in psychopathology. Other postulated indicators of a continuum with schizophrenia include eventual certification and deterioration, an autistic and dereistic life approach, diffuse ambivalence, inappropriate emotional connections and reactions, pananxiety, panneurosis, omnipotent attitudes, subtle thinking disorders, vague contradictory self-presentations, short-lived psychotic episodes, and chaotic sexuality.

Unfortunately, there are no normative data about the uniformity or incidence of these differential clinical signs. Review of their case presentations fails to indicate a basic homogeneity but rather suggests a heterogeneous collection of treatment-refractory patients. Although Hoch and Polatin specifically state that they are not advocating a more refined classification, there is no doubt that the impact of their approach has caused many patients to be labeled "schizophrenic" or "borderline" who would previously have been considered to be suffering from a severe neurosis, affective disturbance, or character disorder. One remembers the wry definition of the "borderline patient" as one who is continually bordering on not paying his bills or not showing up for appointments.

STUDY OF BORDERLINE STATES
BY GRINKER, WERBLE, AND DRYE

Certainly the most ambitious attempt to bring some systematic descriptive inquiry to the concept of "the borderline syndrome" is the volume by Roy R. Grinker, Beatrice Werble, and Robert C. Drye.[1] Their essential stand is that among the patients diagnosed as "borderline" certain ego functions are rather severely impaired, though they do not present cognitive difficulties usually associated with schizophrenia, thus calling for a "borderline" concept. They review the literature on "borderline" and related terms, pointing out the wide variation in usage. The common thread seems to be that the borderline patient falls between neurosis and psychosis.

Grinker and his colleagues deal with terms such as "latent" and "pseudoneurotic" schizophrenia and quote a letter by Paul Hoch indicating that Hoch does not consider the term "pseudoneurotic schizophrenic" equivalent to borderline. The researchers state that "the more specific details of the pseudoneurotic schizophrenia has indicated they are schizophrenic and not what other clinicians have called borderline."[1] However, the basis for this judgment is quite unclear.

They state that apparently the growing attention paid to the borderline diagnosis by psychoanalysts is indicative of the increasing numbers of these patients seen in private practice. However, an alternative to this hypothesis is that the progressive disillusionment of analysts with their ability to make permanent changes in nonpsychotic patients has been masked by terminological revision.

The structural developmental ego defect hypothesized is due to a narcissistic trauma that produces a deficiency in identification processes. Identification is maintained at the infantile level of mimicry and does not reach the secondary level characterized by confidence, independence, and development of regulatory structures. Affectionate relations are sought but feared; loneliness is sometimes defended against by participating with others on an "as-if" level (structured situations are more comfortable than the uncertainty of change); and the sense of identity is woefully weak. The borderline patients to whom Grinker and his associates refer cannot be defined by descriptive symptomatology but only by the inferential ego defect. Nonetheless, the actual operational criteria for their study allows alternative inferences.

The basic criteria for entering the study, whose 51 subjects were young adults, consisted of:

1. Repeated short-term hospitalizations but good psychological functioning in the interim period.

2. Florid, attention-provoking, histrionic episodes preceding hospitalization.
3. Good accessibility during the diagnostic interview or easy possibility for this.
4. Good intellectual contact and intact cognitive functions.
5. Appropriate associations.
6. No systemized delusions or paranoid systems.
7. An ego-alien quality to any transient psychotic-like behavior.

Therefore, entering the study meant operationally that the patient required hospitalization but was not schizophrenic, organic, or toxic; however, the behavior prior to hospitalization was in some sense florid.

One would guess that such criteria would encompass many patients with character or affective disorders. Nonetheless, all such patients were considered "borderline" for this study. Certainly they did not enter the study because they fit the psychological definition proposed by the Grinker group.

My impression of these 51 patients is that they were characterized by marked affective disorder accompanied by disruptive behavior; the predominant affects being anxiety and/or depression.

Data Analysis

Grinker and his associates used the approach of careful observation of patients hospitalized within a research institute for their research. Behavior was rated within an ego psychology framework rather than in symptomatic terms. These ratings were then studied by cluster analysis.

Observations, made primarily by nursing personnel, were for a two-week period, after the patient had been hospitalized about three weeks. Behaviors were translated by coding according to ego function variables using the "Schedule for Individual Ratings of Ego Functions." The schedule had many items lumped under (1) outward behavior, (2) perception, (3) messages, (4) affects and defenses, and (5) synthesis.

For the purposes of cluster analysis, a technique was used that attempts to pick out groups of patients who, when averaged across all measures, are much more like each other than like members of other groups. Unfortunately, this technique may result in several different good equivalent solutions. It does not guarantee, however, that the "best" solution will be found. Also the clusters found will be very much a function of the number and kind of measures used.

The 51 patients had 93 measures. A form of factor analysis, (principle component analysis) was used to reduce these 93 measures to 14 measures that hopefully express what is most common in the original 93 measures. After performing the cluster analysis on the 14 principle components, it was found that the patients could be organized into four groups in a number of ways. However, no one grouping procedure was strongly preferable to any other or, for that matter, highly congruent with any other, a statistically moot situation.

A selection was made on criteria external to the data, i.e., the clinical sense of the groupings as perceived by the authors. Having induced the existence of the four groups on the basis of the 14 common factors, Grinker and his colleagues went back to the original 93 measurements to characterize the selected groups, since characterization in terms of the amalgamated factors would have been incomprehensible.

Group Description

Group 1 in the study is characterized by inappropriate and negative behavior, sloppiness, erratic sleeping and eating, negativism, impulsiveness, and depression. Their outstanding characteristics seem to be pathological affect and affectively laden disruptions of interpersonal relatedness.

Group 2 is also characterized as depressed. However, the members participated in activities and rebelled against the environment. Their outward behavior was vacillating, e.g., vacillating involvement with others, overt anger, depression, and absence of indications of consistent self-identity.

Group 3 presented bland adaptive behavior without evidence of love for anybody or anything. They were withdrawn and intellectualizing, resembling obsessional character disorders. The researchers related this group to the "as-if" disorder.

Group 4 evinced a childlike clinging depression, anxiety, and defects in self-esteem and self-confidence not associated with anger or guilt feelings. The authors recognize in their characteristics a similarity to "neurotic depression."

REVIEW OF PHENOMENOLOGY AND
POSSIBLE DRUG TREATMENT
FOR THE GRINKER GROUPS

Interestingly, three of the four Grinker groups are distinctly characterized as depressed. Further, although Group 3 is not called depressed, their depression score is actually higher than Group 1. Although the four groups are quite arbitrary in their composition, nonetheless it is interesting to review them from the standpoint of syndromal resemblance and possible psychopharmacological intervention.

Group 1 has angry, withdrawn, depressed, and hostile patients. The syndrome of hostile depression treatable with phenothiazines has been supported by J. E. Overall and his associates.[15] The case summary given, however, strongly resembles the hysteroid dysphoric patient described by Donald F. Klein and John M. Davis,[12] who support the use of monoamine oxidase inhibitors.

Group 2 distinctly resembles the extremely labile, vacillating, emotionally unstable character disorder.[16-18] Klein and Davis describe this kind of patient as follows:

> These patients, predominantly adolescents, are frequently treated with intensive exploratory psychotherapy because of their interesting personalities, high degree of interaction with the therapist, marked introspective capacities, manifest psychological distress, and dramatic life experiences. Although capable of forming intense, but brittle, attachments to their therapists and displaying much verbal insight, significant modification of their affective behavior patterns is only occasionally achieved. Many therapists believe, however, that by age 30 these patients are more mature, with or without treatment. These patients' emotionally chaotic states make it impossible for them to utilize their insights or to constructively plan and engage in a career development program.
>
> Phenothiazine medication is distinctly valuable. Interestingly, it alleviates both the high giddy, excitable, impulsive, hedonistic phase and the sullen, hostile, depressive, withdrawn phase. A bland, placid, friendly, and ingratiating manner replaces feelings of confusion, perplexity, anxiety, and depression. Feelings of role diffusion and goal-lessness are reduced without specific solutions being found. During psychotherapy and introspective quality is changed to concern about day-to-day events and peer relationships without marked interest in long-range planning. These patients rejoin their peers in a friendly fashion and are active and popular.
>
> Interestingly, the psychotherapists are often distressed by the change in communications from apparent attempts at insight to minimization, denial and lack of interest in introspection. The therapist will frequently attribute the change in lability to better environmental structuring, ignoring the fact that previous structuring attempts had resulted in negativistic impulsive actions. Therefore, therapists often conclude that medication is interfering with psychotherapy and discontinue it. The patient promptly regresses to

emotional lability and episodic impulsiveness. Patients also encourage medication discontinuation since they usually do not like being on an even keel. They frequently complain of feeling a lack of spontaneity and a certain deadness. However, external behavioral observation of these patients does not bear out their complaints, since they are often active and lively. Their complaints are best understood as expressions of regret that they no longer experience their high giddy periods. In a sense these patients are addicted to their elated stages, miss them and derogate their comparatively normal states. It is also possible that the phenothiazines actually do produce a feeling tone somewhat different from normal for these patients during their even periods. Because of this, these patients will frequently discontinue medication surreptitiously.

Thioridazine, in doses approximating 300 mg hs, has proven most effective and acceptable in this patient group. Larger doses are rarely necessary. It is our impression that nonaliphatic phenothiazines, such as trifluoperazine and fluphenazine, occasionally produce irritability in these patients. On the other hand, they are often effective and have a somewhat lower degree of lethargy associated with their use.

In a double-blind placebo-controlled study Arthur Rifkin and his colleagues[18] demonstrated that lithium carbonate was of distinct value in damping mood swings.

Interestingly, antidepressants have diverse effects in this group. Some patients respond very well with a marked increase in affective stability, whereas others become increasingly angry, irritable, and aggressive, although manic episodes are rare. These effects may also occur in sequence.

It is interesting that the Grinker researchers consider the labile Group 2 to be the core borderline state. A follow-up study of labile patients headed by Rifkin[16,17] indicates that this group of patients, frequently considered schizophrenic by their hospital psychiatrists, in fact had a relatively benign course as did the borderline patients in the Grinker study.

Group 3 patients seem schizoid, obsessional, detached, and withdrawn although they are adaptive and remain adaptive at follow-up. It is not clear what brought them into the hospital in the first place. The relevance of medication for this group is obscure. If they represent a phasic depression in a relatively well-integrated person, antidepressants may be helpful.

Group 4 patients appear similar to neurotic depressives, as the

Grinker group state, in that their behavior is clinging, anxious, and depressed. However, the case example presented only appears passive and dependent. Anxiety is not manifest, although the group is described as clearly anxious. These patients appear to resemble the phobic anxious patients described by Klein[5,6,13] who respond well to imipramine. Since Grinker's study ignores symptoms, it does not isolate specific phobias and phobic dependent manipulations. Therefore, it is impossible to tell whether the resemblance I discern between his Group 4 and phobic anxious patients is actually correct.

In sum, reviewing the various patient descriptions of the Grinker group, I am forcibly struck by the ubiquity of anxious and depressive states associated with maladaptive interpersonal tactics. The assertion that the key is an ego defect seems unsupported by their data.

It is difficult to say whether patients are suffering from too much emotion or too little control. One possibility is that such patients are actually suffering from a system defect in cybernetic self-regulation.[4,9]

PSYCHOPHARMACOLOGICAL STUDIES OF THE PSEUDONEUROTIC PATIENT

The importance of affective derangement in borderline patients is further underscored by psychopharmacological studies. I know of no such studies specifically in the area of the "borderline" patient. There are two studies of patients referred to as "pseudoneurotic" schizophrenics. Both studies involve comparison of phenothiazine and antidepressant medication. Further, each study allows the contrast of pseudoneurotic patients with other schizophrenic patients.

In the study by David L. Hedberg and his collegues[2] the patients were diagnosed as chronic undifferentiated or acute undifferentiated schizophrenics. Overlapping both these groups was a subgroup of pseudoneurotic schizophrenics. Each patient was treated for three eight-week periods, receiving either trifluoperazine, tranylcypromine (an MAO inhibitor), or the combination of tranylcypromine and trifluoperazine. The interesting finding is that 50 percent of the pseudoneurotic schizophrenics responded best to tranylcypromine alone. This was not the case with the other schizophrenics who did not respond as well to this antidepressant medication ($p < .01$).

In my study[6,7] a significant drug-placebo difference in favor of imipramine was shown but not for chlorpromazine with regard to global improvement. Pseudoneurotic schizophrenics did not manifest Kraeplinian signs of schizophrenia. However, they showed massive anxiety, obsessive-compulsive symptoms and adaptations, somatic preoccupations, anhedonia, and frequent agitation to the point where they appeared psychotic. It is common clinical practice in the United States to diagnose such patients as pseudoneurotic schizophrenics. In my study 89 percent of the patients diagnosed pseudoneurotic schizophrenic by the research psychiatrist were also independently considered schizophrenic, in various subcategories, by the hospital staff psychiatrists, thus demonstrating good clinical reliability. However, I hope to show that clinical reliability is no guarantee of validity; rather it may be simply shared prejudice.

In childhood the patients in the study had a frequent history of being shy, dependent, and obedient, with phobic-anxious features. However, they could socialize in unthreatening circumstances and could be emotionally involved with peers and relatives.

Imipramine produced an increased proportion of positive outcomes when compared with placebo, 69.2 percent (9/13) versus 25.0 percent (3/12), respectively (p < .03). Although chlorpromazine showed a trend toward beneficial effects, this failed to reach statistical significance.

Compared with placebo, neither drug produced a significantly different incidence of negative qualitative outcomes.

Reduction of agitated depression occurred significantly more often in the chlorpromazine-treated group than in the placebo-treated group, respectively 42.9 percent (3/7) versus 0 percent 0/12) (p < .04). This qualitative chlorpromazine effect is not specific to pseudoneurotic schizophrenia since it occurred in 12.9 percent (12/93) of all other chlorpromazine-treated diagnostic groups as opposed to 2.3 percent (2/86) of placebo-treated patients in other diagnostic groups (p < .02). It should be noted that the specific usefulness of chlorpromazine in producing reduction of agitated depression in this group of pseudoneurotics was missed in the analysis of the proportion of all positive outcomes.

Mood elevation is the predominant positive effect of imipramine in this diagnostic group, but it just fails to reach statistical significance when compared to placebo.

No change occurred in only 20 percent (4/20) of the drug-treated subjects as opposed to 75 percent (9/12) of the placebo-treated group (p < .003).

The success of the antidepressants in pseudoneurotic schizophrenics should lead us to rethink the entire relationship of these syndromes.

ORDERING EFFECT OF DRUGS ON
PSYCHIATRIC DATA

Certain aspects of drug treatment deserve emphasis as being peculiarly useful in the attempt to understand psychiatric patients. Each patient presents a welter of unique familial relationships, developmental idiosyncracies, social aberrations, affective states, cognitive abilities, symptoms, defects, and maladaptations. The information overload upon the diagnostician is so acute that he is often led to premature closure and scotomization of the data. Furthermore, since the clinician is usually confronted with a cross-sectional picture, it is very difficult for him to know which manifest pathological features are primary, in the sense of being tightly linked to the fundamental disturbances, and which features are secondary, in the sense of being inconstant accompaniments or sequential reverberations.

As R. S. Ledley and S. B. Lusted[14] point out, the fundamental formula of medical diagnosis is "if medical knowledge E is known, then if the patient presents symptoms G, he had diseases f." Conversely, "if diseases f are cured then the patients' symptoms will disappear." Unfortunately for the neatness of this formulation it does not distinguish reversible symptoms from irreversible effects. The persistence of painful, ineffective, and maladaptive affects, thoughts, beliefs, and behaviors in psychiatric patients, long past the period when the apparently initiating causes have ceased to operate, is one of the core problems in pathogenetic theory. If this persistence is due to a variety of causes rather than some unitary repetition compulsion, it is possible that the identification of drug effects that terminate some persisting difficulties, ameliorate others, and are infective in still others may aid us in approaching this aspect of pathogenesis systematically. "Curative" drug therapy would allow us to determine which of the manifold aspects of the patient are symptoms of the illness and which aspects are irrelevant to the illness.

LONGITUDINAL ANALYSIS

One aspect of diagnosis that is often insufficiently attended to is the importance of the extended time sequence of pathological manifestations. Diagnosis in general medicine is never restricted to cross-sectional evaluation; it depends heavily on history. Most computer attempts at diagnosis have utilized either cross-sectional examinational material or historical data (e.g., age of onset) as entries in a multiple-regression analysis that cannot use information derived from longitudinal ordering.

Although change scores may be used as items, extended sequences cannot be put into this form. This issue has probably not been handled adequately because of the unmanageably large number of sequences generated by a combinatorial approach.

Also sequential order may be more important than the exact timing of phases. With a form that samples the patient's history at fixed intervals, the described order of the phases will vary depending on the synchrony of the sampling period with disease periodicity. One might have a patient who was functioning relatively normally until he had a three-month period of emotional lability, followed by a one-month period of elation, followed by a three-month period of depression, perplexity, and withdrawal, culminating in a referential and delusional psychotic state. If one were to use a fixed-time sampling period (e.g., a patient description every six months), quite different orders (e.g., normal depressed psychotic, normal manic psychotic, normal labile depressed psychotic, and so on might be generated, depending on the date taken as the zero point. Such long-period fixed-time sampling approaches become less appropriate the more one is attempting to capture a variable course.

One approach to this problem would be to formalize the descriptive psychiatric knowledge of disease courses in the form of modal sequential descriptions. The course of each patient could be rated for the overall degree it approximates known longitudinal patterns. Allowance would be made for missed phases, and attention would be paid to qualitatively unique aspects and sequences. Discrepancies would be noted, and cases that did not approximate known patterns would be investigated for new patterns. This diagnostic program would emphasize an interplay between the substantiation or contradiction of past beliefs and new inductive attempts rather than a de novo inductive attempt.

The relevance of this discussion of the methodology of handling ordered sequential data to the study of the relationship of drug effects to diagnosis is that the problem of analyzing history is formally identical to the problem of analyzing the time course of drug effect. Present psychopharmacological studies are typically before-and-after two-point studies, with the examiners often completely out of contact with the patient during the intervening treatment period. The only sequence handled is from before to after, and the intervening changes remain unobserved and unanalyzed. As long as the field was preoccupied with the overriding question of proving therapeutic efficacy, the use of before-and-after controlled studies was rational and efficient. Since we are now shifting to the more refined question of which drug for which patient, we must correspondingly refine and intensify our methods, possibly using modal sequential drug-change patterns. This effort will require the intensive longitudinal study of the individual patient by the trained psychiatric clinician. He remains our only presently available tool able to recognize multivariate patterned sequences, either by comparison with specified modal sequences or inductively from atypical courses. The current organization of research into studies with large numbers of patients with brief cross-sectional examinations does not encourage such work. Even the most intensive, ambitious, scientific, and well-organized programs, such as the collaborative studies of the Veterans Administration and the National Institute of Mental Health, do not deal directly with the question of sequential historical and drug-effect analysis, although they point in this direction.

Furthermore for many patient groups, especially those with periodic activation-affective dysregulation, the impact of drugs may be to accelerate the natural course of recovery from the illness. Therefore, in the short space of several months one is given the unusual opportunity of getting an overview of a naturally much longer process, thus allowing the sharp delineation of longitudinal patterns that would otherwise be obscured by life's vicissitudes and the usual difficulties of prolonged longitudinal observation. Critical test of this hypothesis of an isomorphism between the course of both natural recovery and drug treatment would require analyses similar to those outlined above.

These analyses would require the integrated services of a research team of skilled psychiatric clinicians, psychologists, social workers, and statisticians. Furthermore, such studies could only be carried out in an inpatient setting that would welcome and support research programs rather than consider them interferences with the clinical process. It would appear that such intensive studies will require the development of clinical research centers devoted to the specific problem of diagnosis. The Grinker study is an important step in this direction.

PROBLEMS IN SYNDROMAL ANALYSIS

A major difficulty in syndromal analysis is the low status of affective state as an independent variable in psychodynamic theory. Drive states are considered the basic reality. Affects are viewed primarily as merely expressions of drives either in action or blocked or as defenses against drive states, i.e., depression is a defense against aggression.

This deemphasis of affective state as an independent variable in analysis is quite understandable since dynamic theory has derived from the therapeutic endeavors of psychotherapists who had no method for directly affecting the patient's emotional state except insofar as the emotional state was reactive to fantasies, transferences, interpretations, interpersonal relationships, and so forth. Quite understandably, then, the patient's emotional state was viewed as an epiphenomenon since the therapist's focus was on the patient's character and intrapsychic conflicts. Therefore, peculiar repetitious behavior was viewed in the framework of the patient's defective character, repetition compulsion, and/or ego defect. The possibility that the peculiar behavior might be an attempt to express or cope with recurrent intolerable affective states and reactions could not be handled in this dynamic framework.

It is only with the development of pharmacological agents, whose mode of action seems to be the direct amelioration of disordered affects and activation states, that character and ego defect are seen as more secondary than primary. For instance, the patient with an emotionally unstable character disorder who takes lithium still has exploitative and impulsive adaptations; yet it seems far easier to understand these adaptations as being historically secondary to his constantly fluctuating emotional state than the other way around. Similarly, the phobic anxious dependent patient who responds to imipramine by cessation of panic still maintains a phobic dependent manipulative adaptation until he becomes convinced that the panic attacks will not recur; then the ego state shifts to more adaptive procedures. Again, it is the activation-affective disorder that results in the characterological "ego" peculiarities rather than vice versa. Also, character disorders complicated by retarded depressions have responded very well to imipramine with a decrease in hostile exploitative withdrawal.[6]

CONCLUSION

The so-called "borderline state" is an extremely heterogeneous mixture. The phenomenological dissection of this group has been markedly impaired by the primary emphasis on ego structures and identificatory difficulties, i.e., soft thought disorder and characterological peculiarities. In contrast, focusing upon the patient's longitudinal affective status with special emphasis on reactivity or lack of reactivity of his affective swings, as well as the specific nature of the stimuli engendering reactive swings, appears to be a superior strategy.

Further, response to medication plays a key role in the isolation of homogeneous subgroups. Such treatment responses were crucial to the discernment of the phobic anxious patient, the emotionally unstable character disorder, and the hysteroid dysphoric. Application of this systematic strategy of pharmacological behavioral dissection is extremely promising. The two approaches of concentrating on patient affectivity and their responses to medication dovetail neatly. A major problem is the development of adequate institutional facilities for pursuit of these objectives in the nonpsychotic patient.[8,10,11]

REFERENCES

1. Grinker RR Sr, Werble B, Drye RC: The Borderline Syndrome. New York, Basic Books, 1968
2. Hedberg DL, Houck JH, Glueck BC: Tranylcypromine-trifluperazine combination in the treatment of schizophrenia. Am J Psychiatry 127:1141–1146, 1971
3. Hoch PH, Polatin P: Pseudoneurotic forms of schizophrenia. Psychiatr Q 23:248–276, 1949
4. Klein DF: Behavioral effects of imipramine and phenothiazines: Implications for a psychiatric pathogenetic theory and theory of drug action. Recent Advances Biol Psychiatr 7:273–287, 1964
5. Klein DF: Delineation of two drug-responsive anxiety syndromes. Psychopharmacologia 5:397–408, 1964
6. Klein DF: Importance of psychiatric diagnosis in prediction of clinical drug effects. Arch Gen Psychiatry 16:118–126, 1967
7. Klein DF: Psychiatric diagnosis and a typology of clinical drug effects. Psychopharmacologia 13:359–386, 1968
8. Klein DF: Non-scientific constraints on psychiatric treatment research produced by the organization of clinical services, in Merlis S (ed): Non-Scientific Constraints on Medical Research. New York, Raven Press, 1970
9. Klein DF: Psychotropic drugs and the regulation of behavioral activation in psychiatric illness, in Smith WL (ed): Drugs and Cerebral Function. Springfield, Ill., Charles C. Thomas, 1970
10. Klein DF: Approaches to measuring the efficacy of drug treatment of personality disorders: An analysis and program, in Principles and Problems in Establishing the Efficacy of Psychotropic Agents. Publ No 2138. US Dept Health, Education and Welfare, Public Health Service, 1971, pp 187–204
11. Klein DF: Drug therapy as a means of syndromal identification and nosological revision, in Cole JO, Friedhoff AJ (eds): Psychopathology and Pharmacology. Baltimore, The Johns Hopkins University Press, 1973
12. Klein DF, Davis JM: Diagnosis and Drug Treatment of Psychiatric Disorders. Baltimore, Williams & Wilkins, 1969
13. Klein DF, Fink M: Psychiatric reaction patterns to imipramine. Am J Psychiatry 119:432–438, 1962
14. Ledley RS, Lusted LB: Reasoning foundations of medical diagnosis. Science 130:9–21, 1959

15. Overall JE, Hollister LE, Meyer F, Kimbel L Jr, Shelton J: Imipramine and thioridazine in depressed and schizophrenic patients. Are there specific antidepressant drugs? JAMA 189:605–608, 1964
16. Rifkin A, Levitan SJ, Galewski J, Klein DF: Emotionally unstable character disorder: A follow-up study. I. Description of patients and outcome. Biol Psychiatry 4:65–79, 1972
17. Rifkin A, Levitan SJ, Galewski J, Klein DF: Emotionally unstable character disorder: A follow-up study. II. Prediction of outcome. Biol Psychiatry 4:81–88, 1972
18. Rifkin A, Quitkin F, Carrillo C, Blumberg AG, Klein DF: Lithium carbonate in emotionally unstable character disorders. Arch Gen Psychiatry 27:519–523, 1972

James F. Masterson

7

The Splitting Defense Mechanism of the Borderline Adolescent: Developmental and Clinical Aspects

James F. Masterson has applied the borderline concept to the understanding and treatment of a group of adolescent patients who demonstrate severe developmental fixations. Masterson considers these adolescents to have had an arrest of ego development in the separation-individuation phase (18 to 36 months), as described by Margaret Mahler, and they have failed to integrate the positive and negative aspects of the internalized maternal figure into a whole object. Masterson finds Kernberg's concept of splitting useful in describing the defense mechanism these adolescents employ in maintaining the separateness of the maternal image.

Masterson describes the hospital treatment of a 15-year-old girl in which limit-setting and interpretive approaches were used to overcome the splitting defense and the patient's tendency to project the elements of her internal conflicts on to her parents and members of the hospital staff. In Masterson's approach, the parents are also offered psychotherapy but as a separate aspect of the treatment.

The crucial psychopathology of the borderline patient is the defects in ego functioning that are produced by the developmental arrest or ego fixation.[8,10,20,30,35] Much clinical evidence is accumulating to indicate that this fixation occurs in the separation-individuation phase of development—the rapprochement subphase (age 16 to 25 months).[3,4,9,17,28,31,33,35,37,38] The theory to explain the complicated series of events (the mother's withdrawal of supplies at the patient attempts to separate and individuate) that produce this fixation is beyond the scope of this chapter and is presented in great detail elsewhere.[28] This chapter focuses on two important psychopathological consequences of the ego fixation—(1) the persistence of the defense mechanism of splitting and (2) the associated failure of the superego to develop. This psychopathology is best understood from the perspective of normal development as described by object-relations theory.[1,5−7,18,19,21−27,30,34]

NORMAL DEVELOPMENT:
AN OBJECT-RELATIONS VIEW

Object-relations theory can be defined as the psychoanalytic approach to the internalization of interpersonal relations or the study of how interpersonal relations determine intrapsychic structure.

An object-relations unit is an intrapsychic structure derived from the internalization of an interaction with a person. It is composed of a self-representation and an object representation together with the affect that links the two.[11,12]

Early in life, based on the groundwork of the various kinds of care he receives as an infant (being fed and kept warm, and so forth), the growing child constructs a part image of the mother as positive, loving, affectionate, and rewarding, and a part image of the self as being a good child. These two part images are connected by the affect of being cared for, loved, and fed, and of receiving supplies—i.e., the child feels "good." In other words, this type of interaction with the mother begins to form a mosaic or pattern of part self-representation and part object representation through the mechanism of introjection. We say that this contact with the mother has been internalized.[21] However, this is only half of the story.

The child's intense oral dependency and his need for affection and approval from his mother to build ego structure and grow are so absolute and his rage and frustration at the inevitable deprivation of these very supplies on the part of the mother are so great that he feels that the rage may destroy her and himself. To deal with this frustration and anxiety the child develops another object-relations part unit, which consists of the part image of the frustrating, angry, depriving mother and a self-image of being bad and hateful, connected by the affect of depression and rage—i.e., the child feels "bad." In other words, in order to deal with his fear of his rage and to preserve the feeling of receiving supplies from the Good Mother, the child develops two object-relations part units—one positive and one negative. On this basis he relates to people as part objects either all-good or all-bad, all-gratifying or all-frustrating. These two part units remain conscious, but they are kept from influencing one another by the defense mechanism of "splitting."

Splitting can be defined as a primitive defense mechanism that deals with anxiety by keeping separate two opposite affective states. Both states remain conscious, but they do not influence one another. Splitting also keeps separated the internalized self-representation and object representations that are closely linked with these affective states.

The relative weakness and immaturity of the child's ego in conjunction with the immensity of his needs may explain why this defense mechanism is probably employed by all children until around the close of the separation-individuation phase of ego development (about 36 months). Mastery of this growth phase brings with it two crucial dividends: repression comes to supplant splitting as the principle defense mechanism, and there is integration of the two object-relations part units (one positive and one negative) into one whole unit, both positive and negative.

The strengthening of the ego that occurs at this time enables the more sophisticated and effective defense mechanism of repression to supplant splitting as the principal means of dealing with anxiety.[8-10]

At the same time the integration of the two part units into one whole unit enables the child now to relate to people as wholes, both good and bad, gratifying and frustrating the integration also enables him to have this relationship persist despite frustration at the hands of the object.[21,32]

These two key characteristics—the use of repression and the capacity for object constancy[2] so essential for later adjustment and satisfying interpersonal relationships do not develop in the patient with the borderline syndrome.

CLINICAL EFFECT OF SPLITTING

The developmental failure of the patient with a borderline syndrome results in a persistence of the two separate object-relations part units— one positive and one negative—as well as a persistence of the defense mechanism of splitting (paranoid position of Melanie Klein).[13-16] The images of the bad and good mother are never integrated into one whole object, and repression does not come to supplant splitting as a principle means of dealing with anxiety. The patient does not relate to people as one whole object but as if they were part objects, i.e., either good and gratifying, or bad and frustrating; nor does his relationship persist in the presence of frustration. In other words, he does not achieve the depressive position described by Klein.[13-16]

To summarize, the borderline patient has both a fixated, poorly developed, immature ego structure, whose principal defense mechanism is splitting, and an immature poorly developed superego structure with a failure to integrate positive and negative object-relations part-units into one whole unit.

The following example describes the clinical effects of splitting on the present illness, the past history, the transference relationship, and the course of treatment of a 15-year-old girl, Jean.

Chief complaint: "I ran away from home."

Present Illness

Eighteen months prior to admission, while vacationing in Florida, Jean's life-long friend, Amy, appeared at Jean's house dressed in a low-cut dress and was verbally abused by Jean's father, who called Amy a tramp and a whore. He objected to Amy socializing with Jean, which confused and angered Jean. Despite her father's objections she continued to socialize with Amy and her friends on her return from vacation. Over the next several months there were increasing fights between Jean and her father because she associated with friends her father disapproved of, broke curfews, and dressed in a manner to which he objected. If her father forbade her to wear dungarees, she would sneak them out in her purse. During this period Jean and Amy were sent home from school for smoking. Jean began to use marijuana and occasionally to act out sexually.

There were increasing confrontations between Jean and her father during which he accused her of being a slut and a whore and at times slapped her. He objected particularly to her association with Amy, whom Jean describes as being "all screwed up and taking all kinds of drugs." On one occasion, two weeks prior to her admission, Jean's father picked up the phone and found that Amy was talking to his daughter. He told Amy to stop talking to his daughter and not to call again. The next morning Jean sneaked out of the house with Amy and ran away to Chicago where both girls stayed with a friend. Jean's father traced them, contacted the Chicago police, and arrived himself six hours later. After this episode Jean was hospitalized.

The history of present illness as well as the initial interview were inundated by Jean's rage at her father and by the constant conflict with him. Her mother was portrayed at that time as a positive supportive figure: "My mother is the opposite of my father, very giving and understanding. I could see nothing good in my father. . . . My mother and I had a good relationship. I know I could go to her and talk. With my father I'd go beserk—yelling, screaming, and talking about killing him."

Jean dealt with her anxiety about her rage at the frustrating mother—the negative object-relations part unit—by splitting and projection: she retained and projected on her own mother the image of the good mother (positive object-relations part-unit), and she projected the image of the frustrating mother—the negative object-relations part unit—with the associated rage upon the father. This projection was fostered by the father's behavior, most of which was unconsciously prompted by the mother, and by the fact that the father was the unconsciously sanctioned target for the hostility of the entire family.

Past History

Early evidence of the splitting defense was revealed in Jean's past history. She was the second of four children. When Jean was eight, the mother became depressed over severe conflicts with the father. At the same time she had a baby that was born deaf and required most of the mother's time and attention. Jean felt abandoned by her mother, withdrew from her, and displaced her positive object-relations part unit on her next sister Sue (age 18) while continuing to project the negative side on the father: "I guess Sue was the only person who really cared for me and really showed it."

Psychotherapy

The therapist began treatment by setting limits to her acting out, Jean further revealed her defense of splitting by becoming angry and demanding—not with her therapist who ordered these restrictions but with the nursing staff who carried them out. She maintained that her doctor, like Sue and her mother before Sue, was the positive object-relations part unit, i.e., "the man on the white horse who takes care of me."

The nurse on the other hand received the negative object-relations part unit: "I just really got mad at that nurse. I thought about ripping her up and stomping on her. She's just so cold and impersonal. You're the person I'm closest to, doctor. When I don't have my parents here, I have my doctor. I want you to be my good doctor."

Jean preserved her feeling of receiving emotional supplies by splitting the positive and negative object-relations part units, projecting the positive part unit on the doctor and the negative on the nurse.

The splitting maneuvers of the borderline adolescent are ubiquitous. The staff tends to unconsciously identify with the patient's projections to an extraordinary degree. Careful attention must be paid and special precautions must be taken to guard against the splitting producing all kinds of conflicts within the staff about management. A staff member overlooking the patient's splitting mechanisms may identify with negative projections and get into active conflict over management with a staff member who has identified with the patient's positive projections. On this basis, prolonged battles can arise between nurse and therapist, nurse and nurse, therapist and supervisor, administrator and supervisor. To contain, minimize, and deal with the patient's splitting, the therapist must have regular and constant contact with the nursing staff and regular conferences must be held with all care-taking personnel.

In psychotherapy the patient's splitting maneuvers are confronted. For example, the therapist says to the patient, "The nurse is here to help you with your problem. Why do you feel she's attacking you?" Investigations are then made as to the possible reasons for the patient's feeling of being attacked. During this early testing phase of therapy, however, no effort is made to make a psychodynamic interpretation about the splitting. Later on in psychotherapy during the working-through phase a psychodynamic interpretation is made of the patient's splitting mechanism.

Jean's projection of the positive object-relations part unit earlier in life on Sue as the caring mother was interpreted during the working-through phase as a defense against her hostility toward her mother for the abandonment. It was further interpreted that she was now substituting a similar projection on the therapist for the previous projection on Sue and that the nurse was receiving the projection of the negative object-relations part unit that the father had received in the past. These interpretations overcame the splitting defense as evidenced by the fact that Jean immediately became severely depressed and angry and, prompted by guilt feelings, made a suicidal attempt saying, "I guess I felt Sue was one of the only people who really cared for me. I latched on to her, and I didn't want to let go."

After the suicidal attempt Jean, still unable to face the anger at her mother, shifted the projection of the negative object-relations part unit from the nurse to her therapist: "I just realized where I was. I couldn't turn to Sue any more, and I was finally on my own, all alone. I couldn't take that. Nobody else was there but me. First I hated you, my doctor, and then finally my parents and everybody." When the therapist finally confronted her with her last splitting defense, the anger returned to the original object from which it had been split, the mother. The patient could now work through her suicidal depression and homicidal rage at the mother's abandonment.

SUMMARY

This chapter describes two important psychopathological consequences of the ego fixation of the borderline patient—the persistence of the defense mechanism of splitting and the associated failure of the superego to develop. Splitting can be defined as a primitive defense mechanism that deals with anxiety by keeping separate two opposite affective states. Both states remain conscious but do not influence one another. The images of the bad and good mother are not integrated into one whole object, and splitting continues to be the principal means of dealing with anxiety. The example given describes the clinical effects of splitting on the present illness, past history, the transference relationship, and the course of treatment of a 15-year-old girl.

This schematic chapter obviously cannot encompass all the complex factors associated with the splitting defense mechanism in the borderline patient. It attempts briefly to show how careful observations of the patient's splitting mechanisms enables the therapist to understand, predict, anticipate, and cope with the patient's resistances to confronting and working through the patient's rage at the mother.

In the testing phase of treatment the therapist confronts the patient with the unrealistic nature of her splitting and her projections and investigates why the patient feels this way without attempting to interpret the defensive function or psychodynamic origin of the splitting. Later, in the working-through phase of treatment, these latter aspects are interpreted as they reveal themselves in interviews. This latter interpretation of the splitting defense produces great anxiety and mobilizes and returns to its source the affect against which it had been a defense— i.e., rage and depression. Understanding and management of this defense mechanism is one of the keys to successful treatment of the borderline patient.

REFERENCES

1. Fairbairn WRD: An Object-Relations Theory of the Personality. New York, Basic Books, 1954, pp 82–179
2. Fraiberg S: Libidinal object constancy and mental representation. Psychoanal Study Child 24:9–47, 1969
3. Geleerd ER: Borderline states in childhood and adolescence. Psychoanal Study Child 11:336–351, 1956
4. Giovacchini PL: Effects of adaptive and disruptive aspects of early object relationships and later parental functioning, in Anthony E, Benedek T (eds): Parenthood. Boston, Little Brown, 1970
5. Guntrip H: Personality Structures and Human Interaction. New York, International Universities Press, 1961
6. Guntrip H: Schizoid Phenomena, Object Relations and the Self. New York, International Universities Press, 1969
7. Jacobson E: The Self and the Object World. New York, International Universities Press, 1964
8. Kernberg OF: Borderline personality organization. J Am Psychoanal Assoc 15:641–685, 1967
9. Kernberg OF: The treatment of patients with borderline personality organization. Int J Psychoanal 49:600–619, 1968
10. Kernberg OF: A psychoanalytic classification of character pathology. J Am Psychoanal Assoc 18:800–822, 1970
11. Kernberg OF: Early ego integration and object relations. Paper presented at Conferences on Patterns of Integration from Biochemical to Behavioral Processes, New York Academy of Sciences, New York, May 5, 1971

12. Kernberg OF: New developments in psychoanalytic object-relations theory. Paper presented at the 58th Annual Meeting of the American Psychoanalytic Association Washington, D. C., May 1971

13. Klein M: The Psychoanalysis of Children. London, Hogarth Press, 1959

14. Klein M: A contribution to the psychogenesis of manic-depressive states, in Jones E (ed): Contributions to Psychoanalysis, 1921–1945. London, Hogarth Press, 1948, pp 282–310

15. Klein M: Mourning and its relations to manic-depressive states, in Jones E (ed): Contributions to Psychoanalysis, 1921–1945. London, Hogarth Press, 1948, pp 311–338

16. Klein M: Notes on some schizoid mechanisms, in Klein M, Heimann P, Isaacs S, Riviere J (eds): Developments in Psychoanalysis. London, Hogarth Press, 1952, pp 292–320

17. Knight RP: Borderline states, in Knight RP, Friedman CR (eds): Psychoanalytic Psychiatry and Psychology. New York, International Universities Press, 1954

18. Mahler MS: Autism and symbiosis: Two extreme disturbances of identity. Int J Psychoanal 39:77–83, 1958

19. Mahler MS: Thoughts about development and individuation. Psychoanal Study Child 18:307–324, 1963

20. Mahler MS: On the significance of the normal separation-individuation phase: With reference to research in symbiotic child psychosis, in Schur M (ed): Drives, Affects, Behavior. II. New York, International Universities Press, 1965, pp 161–169

21. Mahler MS: On Human Symbiosis and the Vicissitudes of Individuation. 1. Infantile Psychosis. New York, International Universities Press, 1968

22. Mahler MS: A study of the separation-individuation process, and its possible application to borderline phenomena in the psychoanalytic situation. Psychoanal Study Child 26:403–424, 1971

23. Mahler MS: On the first three subphases of the separation-individuation process. Int J Psychoanal 53:333, 1972

24. Mahler MS, Furer M: Certain aspects of the separation-individuation phase. Psychoanal Q 32:1–14, 1963

25. Mahler MS, La Perriere K: Mother-child interaction during separation-individuation. Psychoanal Q 34:483–498, 1965

26. Mahler MS, McDevitt JB: Observations on adaptation and defense *in statu nescendi:* Developmental precursors in the first two years of life. Psychoanal Q 37:1–21, 1968

27. Mahler MS, Pine F, Bergman A: The mother's reaction to her toddler's drive for individuation, in Anthony EJ, Benedek T (eds): Parenthood: Its Psychology and Psychopathology. Boston, Little Brown, 1970, pp 257–274

28. Masterson JF: Diagnosis and treatment of the borderline syndrome in adolescents. Confrontations Psychiatriques 7:125–155, 1971

29. Masterson JF: Treatment of the adolescent with borderline syndrome: A problem in separation-individuation. Bulletin of the Menninger Clinic 35:5–18, 1971

30. Masterson JF: Treatment of the Borderline Adolescent: A Developmental Approach. New York, John Wiley, 1972

31. Masterson JF: Intensive psychotherapy of the adolescent with a borderline syndrome. Cuaderno de la ASAPPIA, 3:15–50, 1972

32. Masterson JF, Rinsley DB: The borderline syndrome: The role of the mother in the genesis and psychic structure of the borderline personality, to be published in: International Journal of PsychoAnalysis, Vol. 56, Part 2

33. Rinsley DB: Intensive psychiatric hospital treatment of adolescents: An object-relations view. Psychiatr Q 39:405–429, 1965

34. Rinsley DB: Economic aspects of object relations. Int J Psychoanal 49: 38–48, 1968

35. Rinsley DB: Theory and practice of intensive residential treatment of adolescents, in Feinstein CS, Giovacchini PL, Miller AA (eds): Adolescent Psychiatry. I. Developmental and Clinical Studies. New York, Basic Books, 1971, pp 479–509

36. Rinsley DB: The adolescent inpatient: Patterns of depersonification. Psychiatr Q 45:3–23, 1971

37. Stein A: Psychoanalytic investigation of and therapy in the borderline group of neuroses. Psychoanal Q 7:467–489, 1938

38. Zetzel ER: A developmental approach to the borderline patient. Am J Psychiatry 7:127, 1971

John Zinner and
Edward R. Shapiro

8

Splitting in Families of
Borderline Adolescents

Paul Federn wrote in 1947 that in order to treat borderline cases (he called the disorder that he was describing "latent schizophrenia") it was important to "improve the mental climate of the whole family."[2] Federn advised against discussing the patient's case with other family members except in his presence, lest his suspicions be aroused. Federn and his coworkers did not, however, use a family treatment approach. They sought the cooperation of their patients' families, especially their willingness to endure a long and expensive course of treatment. However, in 1952 Federn still quoted Freud's remark, "How to deal with the family of the patient? I do not know what to say."[3]

In the past several years investigators at the National Institute of Mental Health have begun to treat adolescent patients, many of whom demonstrate the features associated with borderline states, in a family group. John Zinner and Edward R. Shapiro report on the treatment of adolescent borderline patients with their families. They have applied the object-relations theories of Donald W. Winnicott and Otto F. Kernberg to their case material. They stress, in particular, the severe childhood conflicts in relation to separation that are activated in the family unit by the efforts of adolescent children to achieve independence. An adolescent's effort to break away from the family appears to be viewed by the parents as dangerous and destructive, and powerful emotions of hate and rage are evoked. The "borderline" adolescent, for reasons not altogether clear, seems to be the one upon whom the parents' own conflicts over in-

The authors wish to acknowledge the valuable technical assistance of Mrs. Elaine Batchlor and Mrs. Deborah Runkle.

dependence and autonomy come to be focused. Other siblings may be spared.

The splitting phenomenon has been observed by Zinner and Shapiro as well as Masterson. In both hospital and outpatient settings the adolescent's tendency to divide the staff into all-good and all-bad figures or to assign such roles to the parents themselves and to the therapist in the family treatment unit has been documented. The parents, in turn, project onto the "chosen" child polarized, unrealistic self-representations. In the family treatment situation the therapist becomes the focus of the distorted perceptions and projections. This helps him to bring to the attention of the family members the mutually distorted perceptions that they share and to enable family members to work through the developmental conflicts that interfere with the functioning of the whole family unit.

In this chapter the contribution of the family to certain developmental disturbances of the borderline adolescent will be explored. We have observed a variety of family group behavior associated with disturbed adolescents who evidence strong tendencies toward ego splitting. The term "splitting" is used here as Otto F. Kernberg describes it—a sharp dissociation between self- and object representations that are libidinally tinged from those that are colored by unpleasant aggressive tones.[4] Families of adolescents who exhibit splitting demonstrate a tendency toward splitting that parallels that of their borderline adolescent children. Within the family group attributes of "goodness" (providing, gratifying, loving) and "badness" (depriving, punishing, hating) are separated one from the other and parceled out to different members so that each family member appears relatively preambivalent and single-minded in his relation to the troubled adolescent. The family group taken as a whole appears to be a single ambivalent entity, loving and hating, giving and withholding, punishing and rewarding. Individual members, however, act as if they were the very unidimensional, unconflicted, preambivalent objects that their borderline adolescents perceive them to be.

Our observations of families of borderline adolescents in conjoint family therapy corresponds very closely with the formulation by Kernberg[4] of the borderline personality organization as a specific failure in ego development characterized especially by the persistent splitting of "contradictory ego states." The unintegrated ego states of the borderline patient are, according to Kernberg,[7] basically "two polar primitive constellations of self-object-affect disposition," one of which has an "overall pleasurable, rewarding, 'all-good' " affective quality while its opposite state has a "painful, frightening, aggressive, 'all-bad' affective tone." The ego state, Kernberg observes, represents

> the activation of a past (real or fantasied) relationship with significant persons or a combination of such real or fantasied relationships with fantasy formations geared to protect the individual from real or imaginary dangers in such past relationships.[6]

For the most part, Kernberg's analysis of the borderline personality organization deals with the internalized relationship unit—self-image, object image, affective tone—as an intrapsychic given. Kernberg does not investigate the extent to which these "activated relationships" were real or the elaboration of a fantasy, nor does he indicate that this distinction is central to his formulation of structural consequences of splitting or to the treatment plan for the borderline patient. Our work with whole families in interaction leads us to the conclusion that the internalized object relations derive significantly from actual interpersonal events in the individual's relation with the family. The determining interactions occur early in the patient's life and, to a large extent, persist throughout later development. This recognition has important implications for both treatment and prevention.

The persistence of splitting of all-good and all-bad ego states is regarded by Kernberg as a fixation at or regression to an early stage in the development of internalized object relations during which, in a normal developmental sequence, there is a gradual coalescence of good and bad self-images, object images, and their affective links.[7] This process is estimated to occur during the period between the latter half of the first year of life and the end of the second year with continued evolution throughout childhood. The culmination of this process is the formation of an "ego-identity," which in Kernberg's words constitutes

> an integrated self-concept, "surrounded," as it were, by an integrated conception of others, with ongoing modification of self-concept and concept of others in the process of interpersonal relationships.[7]

The failure of this major integrative task is attributed by Kernberg to the "pathological predominance of primitive aggression," the intensity of which threatens the destruction of the loving self- and object images by the hateful ones. Splitting these polar constellations, then, becomes a crucial defensive requirement mitigating "unbearable anxiety and guilt."[7]

What is the origin of the intensified pregenital aggression? Kernberg feels that both constitutional and environmental factors may play a role.[7] In the event of excessive primary aggression the infant may project his own rage onto his mother, producing a paranoid distortion of her behavior and exaggerating the bad self- and object-images. Kernberg "frequently" finds in the history of borderline patients evidence of "extreme frustrations and intense aggression (secondary or primary) during the first two years of life." The parental nurturant factors that Kernberg sees contributing to the coalescence of good and bad internalized relationships is the "mother's tolerance of . . . [the child's] anger and her continuing provision of love."[7] Such constancy on her part may "crucially strengthen the infant's conviction in the strength of the good self and the good object, and decrease his fear over his own aggressive tendencies." This agrees with Donald W. Winnicott's thinking about the depressive position in emotional development.[9] Winnicott regards the infant's achievement of the depressive position, or "stage of concern," as requiring a maternal "holding environment" in which the mother, in repeated daily interactions, "survives" her child's instinctual assaults during "excited" (high drive intensity) states:

> Integration in the child's mind of the split between the child care environment and the exciting environment (the two aspects of mother) cannot be made except by good-enough mothering and the mother's survival over a period of time.[11]

Thus Kernberg, and especially Winnicott, posed a specific maternal task (the provision of a "holding environment" in Winnicott's terms) that is appropriate to the developmental task faced by the infant. It would appear that this parental function must be maintained throughout childhood, since the consolidation of an ego identity is a gradual refining process that extends beyond the coalescence of contradictory ego states associated with the more primitive conceptions of self and object.

The notion of a variety of family group tasks, each appropriate to specific developmental phases of its members, has been advanced by our group in previous reports.[10,12,13] Extending the psychoanalytically derived theory of small groups to the family, developed by Wilfred R. Bion,[1] we have conceptualized two levels of family group functioning. The first, mentioned above, concerns family behavior that is appropriate to developmental issues and tasks within the family. It is regulated primarily by the reality principle and mediated principally through secondary process thinking. With regard to the evolution of an ego identity in the developing child, the family group as a group, not merely its component members, must provide a "holding environment" in which the group itself "survives" the instinctual demands and angry assaults of the child without, in retaliation, cutting off sources of gratification. Failure to accomplish this task prevents the development of the capacity for ego autonomy,[5] ambivalence, mourning, and concern (authentic guilt), all of which are contingent on integration of "good" and "bad" self- and object representations.

In contradistinction to the task-oriented behavior of the family is a level of group functioning that is governed by shared unconscious fantasies and unconscious assumptions generated by instinctual needs and defensive requirements. These unconscious assumptions provide a "hidden agenda" for the family that is likely to interfere with the fulfillment of developmental tasks of its membership. Within the family group the shared fantasies are played out by members who are both implicitly and explicitly assigned roles in the unconscious family drama. The fundamental mechanism of role attribution is projective identification. Members split off disavowed or cherished aspects of themselves and project them onto others within the family group.

These projections govern the family members' perception of and behavior toward one another when family group behavior is dominated by unconscious fantasies. Family members relate toward the projected aspects of themselves in the same manner as they would were these projections internalized. Hence, internalized conflict *within* individuals may be externalized, assuming the form of interpersonal conflict *between* family members.

Frequently the relationship between parents and split-off aspects of themselves projected onto their children replicates the family relations of the parent when he was a child. Our group has reported on the family of an impulsive delinquent adolescent where such reenactment took place.[13] The youngster's mother, by identification with the aggressor, acted as if she were her own austere and punitive mother. Simultaneously she projected her own unintegrated impulses onto her teenage daughter and thereby re-created, with roles reversed, a relationship of conflict first experienced a generation previously.

We have also asserted that there exists a relationship between the severity and primitiveness of an adolescent's psychopathology and certain attributes of projective identification within his family group. Specifically, these family variables are (1) the capacity of parents to experience themselves as separate from particular offspring, (2) the dependence of parental defensive organization on transpersonal defenses, such as projective identification, which tend to require considerable collusive participation of the child, and (3) the content of parental projections, that is, whole or part objects, drive representations, elements of superego. More primitive personality organization in children is fostered by families in which parents have tenuous self-object differentiation, rely heavily on projective identification as a defense, and project whole-object representations rather than, for example, a relatively refined aspect of superego.

Our observations in this chapter focus on unconscious fantasies, unconscious assumptions, and the quality of projective identifications in families with hospitalized adolescents where splitting is a prominent aspect of the youngster's psychopathology. We are explicitly limiting our investigation to the phenomenon of splitting. We recognize that the borderline syndrome encompasses much more than this process, such as a protean symptomatology and diversity of ego deficits.[4] However, the family's contribution to these processes awaits further study.

Our observations involve a group of inpatient adolescents and their families on a residential treatment unit sponsored by the Intramural Research Program of the National Institute of Mental Health. Therapeutic modalities included intensive psychoanalytically oriented individual psychotherapy for the adolescent and occasionally his siblings, weekly conjoint family therapy, and conjoint marital therapy for the parents. In addition, all family members participate in a weekly multiple-family group and the adolescents join in a weekly study group of peer and authority relations. The inpatient service operates in a therapeutic community in which the emphasis is on remediation of learning problems of the patients and continuation of their education.

Many of our adolescent patients have a borderline personality organization in Kernberg's terminology.[4] They fit that classification both descriptively and structurally, that is, with characteristic ego pathology, of which splitting is an integral and prominent feature.

The defensive use of splitting, we have discovered, is not limited to the adolescent patient. It appears, in fact, that the family group is participating with the adolescent in a shared activity that constitutes a regression to a preambivalent state in which different members come to be perceived as unambivalently "good" or "bad." These terms are attributes defined, as in Kernberg, by the affective quality of the relationship at a given moment. "Good" and "bad," therefore, connote not moral evaluations or judgments made by a mature superego but affective states of pleasure and "unpleasure." In these families, sources of gratification and of deprivation of oral supplies are not perceived as emanating from the same family member. For example, a parent–child relation is experienced as "all-good" and gratifying in an idealized fashion only insofar as it is purged of its "bad" or hateful qualities, which are projected into the other parent who is perceived unambivalently as ungiving, hating, and punitive.

An illustration of a frequent family group split follows: A mother claims that her relationship with her disturbed adolescent had always been untarnished and happy. Whatever difficulties there are with the child are seen by both as the fault of the father, who is viewed as hating the youngster and who is hated by her. The "bad" parent colludes in this fantasy no less than any other member by being the one in the family who is always saying no to the children's wishes or attracting hostility through provocative behavior. As our young patient shrewdly noted, "When I go ask my mother [good] for something and she says, 'Go ask your father [bad],' I know *she* doesn't want me to have it." She is observing that her mother cannot bear being perceived as anything but the one providing her with gratification—the "good mother." In reciprocal fashion father becomes, in effect, the "bad mother," acting out mother's "bad" wishes toward her daughter, which mother then experiences vicariously through the father–daughter relationship. This particular woman frequently provoked her husband into beating their daughter and witnessed his actions. She stood by with an agonized expression but made minimal efforts to intercede.

The split within the family of the "good" parent and the "bad" parent is common, but it is by no means the only form in which the dissociation of loving and hating occurs. The family, as a whole, for example, may experience itself as all-good, as the sole competent and caring provider for its adolescent; the outside world, in complementary fashion, is viewed as hostile and dangerous to the adolescent. Similarly, the various children within the family may be delineated in an unambivalently polarized manner. In one family two siblings were explicitly experienced by their parents as "night" and "day." "Day" was seen as caring about the family and giving unselfishly, while "night" was perceived as exploiting the parents, stopping at nothing to provide pleasure for herself at their expense. These parental definitions of their two daughters were highly resistant to efforts by the adolescents to indicate the many ways in which they were, in fact, alike. In another form in which we find splitting, the adolescent views the family as totally resourceless, hateful, and destructive while he experiences his peer group as if the members were a boundless reservoir of caring and nurturance. There are, therefore, a variety of configurations that dissociated attributes of "goodness" and "badness" may take within the family group and its social context. Despite this variability, however, there remains a common denominator in these families: the shared unconscious fantasy of the family group that hostile feelings will destroy the loved anaclitic object. The fantasy generates, then, the defensive imperative for the family to split the loving and hating self- and object representations in order to protect the paramount libidinal ties.

This primitive kind of family group behavior has a number of curious features. The tendency toward overt splitting may not have been typical of the family earlier in its history as a group, and it may continue to wax and wane. The family's use of such primitive defensive operations may also occur in an encapsulated way, most commonly in response to issues involving certain adolescent offspring. In its interaction with siblings and the outside world the family may employ more advanced ego defenses and evidence greater maturity in object relations. In regard, however, to behaviors of *particular* adolescents that herald autonomy and separation, the family as a whole appears to regress toward the use of primitive defensive operations involving splitting. The loss through maturation of certain children is experienced by the family as a hateful abandonment. Independence is not seen, at levels of unconscious group fantasy, as a desirable goal for the adolescent but rather as a rejection and devaluation of the group. The youngster is experienced as leaving the family because he hates it. A fantasy evolves that if the family became more "good" or satisfying to the adolescent and purged itself of those "bad" qualities that cause him to wish to grow up, then perhaps he would, after all, remain. The regressive splitting of "good" and "bad" self-object representations, thus, addresses itself to this family fear of losing the child. With the "badness" projected onto the outside world or into certain family members (such as the "bad" father), who can then be effectively ostracized, it is hoped that the adolescent will be drawn back into the now purified family circle.

What causes the family to respond so regressively to autonomous development of one child while the reaction to the growth of siblings may be relatively benign? The answer lies in the different meanings that each child has for his parents. Early in their life, and often even before birth, certain children are "chosen" by a parent to participate in a reenactment of the parent's own early object relations with his parent. Our earlier example of a mother's vicarious enjoyment of her daughter's delinquency was illustrative. The reactivated object relation there, however, was fixated around a conflict developmentally more advanced than the dyadic themes embodied in the relations of our patient's parents with their family of origin. These themes are (1) the incomplete resolution of a symbiotic tie that the parent experiences as a child[8] and (2) the failure of the parent, as a child, to achieve a stable integration of "good" and "bad" ego states.

It is the borderline adolescent within the sibship who has long held this special meaning for his parents. They have defined or delineated him—by projective identification—as their parent or as themselves as children. Who is to be parent and who is to be child in this reenactment is quite variable over time. Roles within the dyad fluctuate, but the integrity of the reactivated primitive object relation is sustained as is the affective quality of the interaction. This phenomenon is similar to what Kernberg describes as the "oscillating" projections of self- and object representations onto the analyst in the transference developed by borderline patients.[5]

James F. Masterson describes the basic dilemma of the borderline adolescent as a conflict between strivings for autonomy and fear of parental abandonment.[9] He asserts that each of the parents of the borderline adolescent is borderline. Each has failed to resolve their symbiotic tie with their mother; therefore, they respond to their youngster's efforts toward independence by threats to withdraw supplies. This terrifies the adolescent and leads to defensive clinging by him and regression to more primitive ego defenses, including object splitting. Masterson, similarly, observes that the parents see their child as a "person from their past" from whom they were unable to separate. Our experience with many of these parents, however, does not justify considering them as borderline, certainly not in Kernberg's terms. All do, however, have a relatively deficient resolution of symbiosis and formation of an ego identity, and in *relation to the designated child* a striking but limited regression to these fixation points can occur. In addition, the categorical definition of these parents as borderline makes it difficult to explain how many siblings can effect a relatively benign separation from the same parents. Thus, we cannot concur that each and every parent of a borderline adolescent is borderline. What we are stressing is that the borderline quality lies not necessarily in the traits or character of any one or both parents but in the regressive behavior of the entire family group in interaction. This is most manifest in splitting phenomena.

Masterson advances as the "basic psychodynamic theme" of his book his observation that "the borderline mother withdraws emotional supplies at her child's efforts to separate and individuate."[9] This is a crucial and characteristic phenomenon that we likewise have repeatedly observed. In our thinking, however, this retaliatory withdrawal of supplies is only one element rather than the "basic . . . theme" of a general group dynamic of defensive splitting. The borderline adolescent, in effect, is faced in his family with a carrot and a stick. The carrot is the implicit promise of an all-gratifying idealized object relation with certain family members who are purged of all hateful qualities. These "bad" attributes, in turn, have been projected into other family members or into the outside world, which is then seen as hostile and uninviting.

A 17-year-old girl who was making conflicted and halting efforts to feel independent and to live away from home accused her parents of "offering candy to a baby" in their seductive attempts to woo her back by offers of an automobile and special family vacations and by picturing the family as idyllic in contrast to the harsh deprivations in the world that lay outside the warm, giving family circle. This is the carrot, the price of which is the relinquishing of the adolescent's strivings for autonomy.

The stick, on the other hand, represents the family "becoming" the "bad mother" in reaction to their child's attempts to separate. This is a potent retaliatory sadistic group behavior that threatens the total cutoff of supplies and oral ostracism, which is terrifying to the youngster who then equates psychological growth with alienation and starvation. A 15-year-old girl told her family during a conjoint session that she was "getting my head together" in her individual therapy but questioned the value of the family sessions because of her parents' continual angry attacks on the "bad" therapists whom they felt were destroying the fabric of the idealized "good" family. She would prefer, she said, to substitute another individual session for the family meeting. Her father responded in a very threatening tone:

Well, I'm going to caution you, that you better be very careful and think out very carefully and clearly what you're deciding because I feel you're coming to points of decision. The family is an ongoing thing, and it's going to keep on going, and if you want to step aside and not be involved in it, which I firmly believe is your choice. . . .

The stick does not necessarily involve expulsion from the family. The family group may turn its angry reaction against itself by some of its members threatening to die or to become ill should the adolescent pursue his initiatives.

The borderline adolescent is faced with an all-or-nothing choice brought about by the defensive splitting within the family. If he wishes to preserve the idealized primitive all-good self-object relation with the family or some of its members, he must entirely sacrifice his autonomy. If he chooses to progress in his development, he will precipitate himself into the all-bad, punitive, depriving self-object relation with the family group. Navigating between this Scylla and Charybdis is an oppressive burden for the adolescent. This is all the more true because of his fixation points in earlier development around issues of separation-individuation and integration of good and bad self-representation and object representation. Sequelae of these unfulfilled earlier developmental tasks persist in subtle form during latency when there is no impending threat of separation for the family and the positive "good" self-object relations predominate. It is the emergence into adolescence that reactivates the earlier conflicts in the child and, in parallel fashion, reawakens in the family group the potential for a regression to primitive defensive operations. It is the use of these defenses of splitting and projective identification that renders the family unable to provide the requisite "holding environment" while the adolescent attempts to rework and redefine his ties to his original objects.

Within such a family group the choices for the adolescent are threefold: (1) to repudiate personal maturation in order to preserve the "good" object ties; (2) to opt for autonomy with a persisting "bad" self-object relation with the family; and (3) to oscillate between the two in a state of conflict, anxiety, and uncertainty. A fourth choice—developmental progression—can be arrived at through treatment. In our clinical setting we encounter most often the third situation, simply because it is the one most filled with conflict and turmoil—both intrapsychic and interpersonal. Those who choose the second path, that is, to separate, generally are not referred for hospitalization to our center. We do, however, encounter them at times as parents and siblings of our inpatients. It is clear that they have paid a high price for their autonomy since the bad self-object representations predominate and are experienced as severe self-hatred and primitive guilt or a projection of the rage into what is thus felt to be a hostile world (an extension of the hateful expulsive family). The first choice, that of extreme dependency in a "good" relation with the family, also is less familiar among our inpatients, for while the youngster and the family group are both regressed, there is little conflict of the sort that precipitates a search for outside help.

The fourth choice, that provided by treatment, involves a modification of the family's unconscious assumptions toward the development of a "holding environment" in which the adolescent can pursue his autonomous growth without retaliation and object loss.

This absence of the "holding" function in families of our adolescent patients reflects failures in the holding environments of the parents as infants and children. We have commented, for example, on how the adolescent's move toward autonomy may be experienced by parents as a total repudiation of them and of the family, to which they may react with a rage that has prominent vindictive qualities. The parent in this situation is reenacting his early experience of being abandoned by an inconstant parent. His rage is the oral rage of an infant from whom supplies are being withheld. The retaliatory withholding that our parents visit on their adolescent thus constitutes an identification with the aggressor, that is, the parents' "bad" parent. This identification is a defense against the anxiety generated by the unavailability of parental sustenance. In similar fashion, attempts by our parents to idealize their relation with their separating youngster represent attempts to recapture their own experience as infants in relation to the "good" mother. Their idealization is defensive, as we have said, and requires some repository for the projection of split-off, affectively negative self-object relations.

Some excerpts from audiotaped conjoint family sessions will illustrate the dynamic process of splitting within families of borderline adolescents and elucidate unconscious assumptions that determine the family group behavior. Portions from conjoint sessions of two families reflect the threat posed to the group by the improvement in treatment and increasingly age-appropriate independence of their adolescents. Allen, 18 years old, is ending his hospital stay and making plans for discharge:

Excerpt 1

ALLEN	I'm thinking of leaving here and getting an apartment on the outside . . . and I think I've found that . . . for my *own* good, the approval I want is the absence of disapproval.
FATHER	That I don't understand. I don't know what the absence of disapproval means.
MOTHER	Either you approve or you disapprove.
ALLEN	Well, you don't disapprove or don't approve, you can . . .
MOTHER	In other words, you're going to do this regardless of how we feel? Is that it?

Linda, 16 years old, was quoted earlier. It was *her* father who responded to her wish for more individual and less family therapy by threatening her with ostracism. Here she is maintaining that she is feeling better about herself "as a person" and attributes her improvement to her therapeutic program:

Excerpt 2

FATHER	I don't see where she is different now than she was in March 1970. . . . Let's look at the overall activity of the people involved. Linda, directly do you feel that you are being actively involved as a person more so than you were in March of 1970? Now that's a direct question.
LINDA	As a person but not as a family member.
FATHER	And I'm afraid—and I'm afraid I have to agree with you, and I see you developing more as a person but as a person that does not relate—is not related to the family.
MOTHER	Or anybody else.
FATHER	Well, I don't know who she's related to but she's not related to the family. The activities and the things that are uppermost in your goals and aspirations as a person and the things that you

keep on working toward and keep getting reflected back to us
have nothing to do with the family and this may be the way
it's—the way it is. But if it is, I—I—all I can say is I can be
sympathetic to it, but that's all I can be. I can't accept it.

Allen, in seeking to have his own apartment, and Linda, in being
more "actively involved" within herself "as a person," are joining developmental issues appropriate to their age. It was, in fact, their very
shunning of such tasks that brought about their hospitalization. Yet their
parents, in a shared way, react with hurt and anger. They have difficulty
grasping the notion of their children's individuation and persist in viewing
them from a symbiotic perspective. They wonder what Allen could mean
that parents might neither approve nor disapprove. What does Linda
mean about becoming involved within oneself but not within the family?
The "absence of disapproval," in fact, represents the "holding environment" for Allen. Nonetheless, the unconscious assumptions of the group
are that autonomous acts, independent thinking, and differences of
opinion are equated with rejection and abandonment of the family; the
child leaves the family because it is bad. In Winnicott's term, the family
cannot "survive" the emotional growth of the child.[11] The gravity of this
rejection needs to be underscored. It is experienced as if the parents were
being deprived of the wherewithal necessary for their survival.

That this fantasy is shared by the group as a whole is illustrated by
Sharon, who believed that her efforts to extend her world beyond the
family would cause an increase in her diabetic mother's blood sugar
levels, bringing her perilously close to a heart attack. Sharon was admitted to our treatment unit for truancy and failure at school, drug taking,
and intense conflict with her father. These symptoms were of secondary
importance to her parents, however, who saw the hospitalization as an
effort to sequester her from an "all-bad" peer group in order to return
her to the bosom of the "all-good" family. A further defensive splitting
within the family involved a group fantasy that mother was an unambiva-
lent source of gratification for Sharon's needs while father was delineated as the one who, in his own words, is "the bad guy—the one who
takes away." The split was reified by the referring agency who recommended that father not speak to Sharon and that all of the communica-
tions between them be conveyed through mother. During the course of
her treatment Sharon verbalized a wish to live away from home
following her discharge. Her mother became enraged, wanted to "wash
my hands" of Sharon and threatened, in retaliation, that should Sharon
leave home she would not be permitted to return. In the following
excerpt the previous split has been restored, with the mother dissociating

herself from her angry threat and attempting to resurrect her "good"
relationship with Sharon by projecting the "badness" onto the father:

Excerpt 3

DR. A.	What do you feel about your parents' reaction to your talking about your plans and . . .
SHARON	All this time they were thinking that I would want to come home to live.
MOTHER	I'd still like to see you come home to live, Sharon—but if you don't want to—you'd only make our whole family miserable if you did—and try it on your own. And, then if *you* decide that you want to come home—you're welcome at any time. And, if you feel . . .
SHARON	Why don't you say I'm not welcome?
MOTHER	Do you want me to say you're not?
SHARON	Then I would have more motivation to make it. If I—if I—say—if I—just—if—I
MOTHER	The decision to come home has to be *yours*.
SHARON	. . . thought to myself, well—well—anytime I want I can just give up and go home to live. Then—there wouldn't be so much motivation—well, there would be—more than there is.
MOTHER	I think that if I told you you could not come home—you'd find yourself—maybe—against a wall and not know what you want to do. I'm leaving a couple of doors open to you. And I think that's best—I feel that if you want to come home this has to be your decision.
SHARON	But you said a long time ago—you said last year—if you ever move away from home, you're not coming back.
MOTHER	I didn't say that, your father said that.
SHARON	*You* said that.
MOTHER	No I didn't.
SHARON	*You* told me that.
MOTHER	Well, maybe I've changed, 'cause I can't even remember saying it.
SHARON	Do you remember her saying it?
FATHER	Remember *her* saying it? No. [Pause]
SHARON	Do you remember saying it yourself?
FATHER	I remember thinking it—and I might have—ah—touched on it. Yeah.
SHARON	Do you still think that? I mean, do you think that would be a good idea?
FATHER	What?
SHARON	You haven't said—anything about—about me not living at home. [Pause]
FATHER	I mentioned yesterday I can't get used to the idea—I guess it's

mainly because I [pause] have second thoughts about you
doing it—about you being able to do it that way.

In this excerpt it is important to observe the collusion of Sharon and
her father in affecting the split of "good" and "bad" within the family.
With little resistance, father assumes the primary responsibility for
having threatened to expel Sharon from the family should she live away.
He does this despite his having witnessed, in the past, his wife's angry
threats to cut Sharon off. Sharon, meanwhile, with similar facility,
reorients her hostile challenge away from mother and toward father. At
this point the splitting has evolved. Mother, superficially supporting
Sharon's independence, is in a "good" relation with her, while father who
doubts Sharon's ability to "do it that way" becomes the partner in the
bad self-object relation. This is not an unfamiliar role for father. In the
following interaction Sharon has, with considerable anxiety, tried to express her anger at mother for the latter's blind trust and unwillingness to
see problems in her relation with Sharon. In the midst of her efforts to
address her mother, father intrudes as a combatant:

Excerpt 4

FATHER	Well, how about talking about your side of it then?
SHARON	You're—see—you're putting yourself . . .
FATHER	I'm willing to talk about my side of it.
SHARON	. . . in the middle—as soon as Mom was feeling a little pressure you came in and put yourself in the middle—like—like—to try to get all—all the anger from me—that—maybe she was getting at that moment.
DR. A.	You mean, just now, that that was happening?
SHARON	Yeah.
DR. A.	You also were directing your anger. You stopped it, apparently, directing it toward your Mother—and then directed it toward your Father.
SHARON	Sure. He comes in handy.
MOTHER	You mean—you're really angry with *me*?
SHARON	Yeah.
FATHER	Really? Or, or—is, is . . .
SHARON	I have been.
MOTHER	Why?
FATHER	More than me? Or what—I mean—go on—I wish you'd say what you're angry about. And—and—who you're angry at.
SHARON	Why? Because of the way—both of you—the way you sit there and act like everything's going great.
FATHER	No, we're sitting here admitting that things—aren't right.
MOTHER	Why don't you let her finish?

Father, in the excerpt, is essentially competing with mother to be the recipient of Sharon's anger. His motivation to be the target for her hostility is determined by the funneling of his libidinal relation with Sharon into a sadistic mold. During her latency he tickled her buttocks, asking her if she would permit him to continue when she was older. In adolescence the tickling evolved into beatings spurred by jealousy of her interest in boys. Thus his participation as the "bad one" in the family drama is a compromise formation, both satisfying and defending against his erotic interests.

Sharon feels that her father "comes in handy" in helping her deflect her anger from mother. Within the family there is a shared fantasy about the fragility of mother's health and the potentially lethal effect of "upsetting" her. Mother uses her mild diabetes as a way of monitoring and undermining Sharon's attempts to separate. In a typical interaction Sharon returned home late from visiting friends to discover her mother flaunting and devouring a huge piece of cake and ice cream. Sharon expressed her fear that mother was hurting herself, to which mother responded, "What difference does it make? You don't care anyway." The fantasy that mother will be injured by those acts and feelings of her children that displease her has the status of a firm conviction in the family, and its power to generate anxiety in the group cannot be overestimated. Thus, in this family the retaliatory withholding of supplies from the separating adolescent is accomplished both by expulsion ("If you leave, never come back.") and suicidal threats ("If you leave, I will die.").

Excerpt 5 is taken from a session shortly before the mother is to be admitted for a brief, elective medical hospitalization. Sharon's sister, Ruth, has been silent in recent sessions and now expresses her fear of talking in the family:

Excerpt 5

DR. B.	Is that what keeps you a lot from saying what's on your mind, because you fear Sharon's reaction?
MOTHER	(*very assuringly*) You don't have to worry about my reaction.
RUTH	I have to worry about your reaction a lot.
MOTHER	Like what? As much as I have to worry about your reaction?
RUTH	I don't know—I say something here, when we get home "That's not true, you just said that for attention."
MOTHER	How long ago, Ruth?
RUTH	The last time I ever said anything; that's how long ago.
MOTHER	How long ago, how long ago, Ruth?
RUTH	A long time ago.
FATHER	Like what? Can you remember what it was?
RUTH	I don't know. . . . It was something about my parents.

DR. A.	. . . did you make some kind of a promise with yourself that you weren't going to speak again?
RUTH	No, I didn't make a promise. It's just that every time I think of something to say I remember.
DR. A.	What happened, and you don't say it?
RUTH	I remember what has happened before and what will probably happen again.
DR. A.	Is that why you've been so quiet the past couple of months?
RUTH	It wasn't I didn't want to say anything. It's just that I didn't— I'm afraid to say anything.
FATHER	I wish you'd get over that fear.
RUTH	I'm feeling it right now.
FATHER	Why?
RUTH	By the way she's acting.
MOTHER	Who?
RUTH	You.
MOTHER	Me?
RUTH	I feel like as soon as we get out of here you're going to say, "Why were you saying all that?"
MOTHER	I'd like you to come to the point and speak and say what you want. I've told you that many times too.
FATHER	I don't think your feelings are justified, Ruthie.
DR. A.	That's just what Ruth is concerned about . . .
MOTHER	Probably an excuse.
DR. A.	Being told that her feelings are not justified or it's an excuse— I think if she says what she feels she doesn't want to hear that it's an excuse or that it's not justified.
MOTHER	I don't know . . . she's not afraid of upsetting me. Whatever she feels like she wants to tell me, she tells me. She had me all upset today by her comments this morning. [*Begins to cry*]
FATHER	This morning? What did she say?
MOTHER	I told you.
RUTH	What did I say?
MOTHER	Who's going to drive you to school when I'm in the hospital, and how are you gonna sleep in the house by yourself while Daddy's working—get your hands off your face. . . .
FATHER	Ruth, we only have an hour and we're stagnant right now. Why don't we speak up?
MOTHER	(*sharply in trembling voice*) No. I don't know why she's hesitating to say what's on her mind. She doesn't hesitate to tell me what's on her mind, and I don't think she's worried about upsetting me because she didn't think about if it would upset me this morning when she just blurted out to me, "Who's going to drive me to school in the morning and do I have to sleep here at night alone?" I told her I drive her girlfriend to school every morning. Maybe her mother would drive them to

school and that maybe one of the dogs could go upstairs with
her. I don't like the idea of her being alone at night either, but I
don't think it's her worrying about my reaction because she
didn't worry about it this morning because it upset me all day.

RUTH   (*weeping silently*)

MOTHER   Ruthie, move your hair away from your face and talk—would
you please?

FATHER   Ruth, I don't like to see you sitting there with your face
masked either, come on.

Here the family is paying lip service to the therapeutic "task" of
saying what one feels. Both parents exhort Ruth to speak up without
worrying about their reaction. They delineate her as unjustifiably fearful
of retaliation, which, if it ever occurred, did so in the remote past. A
contradictory injunction, however, reinforces Ruth's anxiety about
speaking. Ruth does not worry about her mother's reaction *enough*.
After all, if she were so worried, why did she then "say what's on her
mind" that morning and "upset" mother all day? Thus the unconscious
assumption that adolescent individuation is equated with abandonment
of and by the family is acted out in the following sequence: speaking out
is upsetting mother thus raising blood sugar thus causing heart attack
thus losing mother.

Retracing our central themes as they have appeared in these
excerpts, we have seen the families' angry negativistic response to the
adolescents' evolving autonomy (Excerpts 1 and 2). The family engages
in defensive splitting (Excerpt 3) in an effort to create an unambivalently
positive tie which will seduce the adolescent into relinquishing her independent strivings and remain symbiotically bound to the family. This
splitting is a shared group behavior in which even the recipients of the attributes of "badness" actively collude (Excerpt 4) out of their own dynamics of defense. The adolescents' efforts in the direction of separation-
individuation are opposed by fear of losing the "all-good" object
(Excerpts 4 and 5), fear of withdrawal of supplies by the "all-bad" object
(Excerpt 3), and a wish to sustain the infantile symbiotic ties with the seductive "all-good" object (Excerpt 3).

One can observe, however, in Excerpt 3 that Sharon's mother is beginning to accept the possibility of her living away from home. It is only
at face value that this position represents a shift in mother's longing for a
symbiotic tie. Mother must agree with Sharon's wish to leave lest she
disrupt the "good" object relation. Hence she constructs a new fantasy
in which Sharon's departure will bring them closer together:

MOTHER   No, I feel that she'd be concerned or—about—how the family

	is doing. She—I'm sure she'd want to see the family. I—I can't see her wanting to detach herself completely. In fact, I feel
FATHER	I can't either but this is what she—
MOTHER	That if she goes—on her own—I feel that there'll be even more of a closeness—than if she were to come home. I really and truly feel this. I could be wrong.

Simultaneously, the parents' delineation of Sharon as the one who stays at home is passed on to Ruth, three years her junior:

MOTHER	Maybe Ruth won't want to leave home. No, maybe Ruth would like to stay home until she gets married.
SHARON	Maybe. (*pause*)
MOTHER	This would have to be Ruth's decision.
SHARON	I doubt it.

Mother's yearnings for a symbiotic bond survives Sharon's potential geographic separation. Similarly, the family fantasy of having a child who "won't want to leave home" has a permanence that outlasts the group's choice of a particular member to fill that role. The shifting of such a definition from one child to another underscores our thesis that the psychological outcome for the adolescent is a product, to a significant degree, of a transactional process within the family. Clearly the very improvement of one patient creates a new dilemma for her sibling and argues for a treatment program that involves the entire family.

The question might be raised as to whether splitting within the family is a *secondary* consequence of having a borderline adolescent who employs such defenses himself. We regard this issue of what is primary or secondary as spurious in the sense that it connotes a linearity which does not exist in group processes. All of us are born as "splitters"; our task is to integrate. Splitting within the family of the borderline adolescent is determined by a *shared* fantasy that hating destroys the loved object. By not providing a holding environment, the family, no more "causes" (in the directional sense) splitting in the child than the child "causes" (by his potential to love or to hate) splitting within the family. Rather, it is the unconscious assumption of the group as a whole that evokes the regression toward primitive defenses that are common to all but highlighted in some, by their experience, as major points of fixation. The borderline outcome thus represents the failure of a group task.

In summary, we have examined the dichotomized world of internalized object relations of the borderline adolescent from a family group perspective. We have concluded that the adolescent's failure to integrate "good" and "bad" self-object representations is an inherent part of splitting processes within the family as a whole. The defensive operations are founded on the unconscious fantasy that growth and autonomy in children imply rejection and devaluation of the family.

REFERENCES

1. Bion WR: Experiences in Groups. London, Tavistock Publications, 1961
2. Federn P: Principles of psychotherapy in latent schizophrenia. Am J Psychother 1:129–145, 1947
3. Federn P: Ego Psychology and the Psychoses. New York, Basic Books, 1952
4. Kernberg OF: Borderline personality organization. J Am Psychoanal Assoc 15:641–685, 1967
5. Kernberg OF: The treatment of patients with borderline personality organization. Int Psychoanal 49:600–619, 1968
6. Kernberg, OF: New developments in psychoanalytic object-relations theory. Paper presented at the 58th Annual Meeting of the American Psychoanalytic Association, Washington, D. C., 1971
7. Kernberg OF: Early ego integration and object relations. Ann NY Acad Sci 193:233–247, 1972
8. Mahler MS: On child psychosis and schizophrenia: autistic and symbiotic infantile psychoses. Psychoanal Study Child 7:286–305, 1952
9. Masterson JF: Treatment of the Borderline Adolescent: A Developmental Approach. New York, John Wiley, 1972
10. Shapiro R, Zinner J: Family organization and adolescent development, in Miller E (ed): Task and Organization. New York, Wiley, 1975
11. Winnicott DW: The depressive position in normal emotional development, in Collected Papers. Through Pediatrics to Psychoanalysis. New York, Basic Books, 1958
12. Zinner J, Shapiro R: Projective identification as a mode of perception and behavior in families of adolescents. Int J Psychoanal 53:523–529, 1972
13. Zinner J, Shapiro R: The family group as a single psychic entity: Implications for acting out in adolescence. Int Rev Psychoanal 1:179–186, 1974

John T. Maltsberger and
Dan H. Buie

9

The Psychiatric Resident,
His Borderline Patient, and
the Supervisory Encounter

However we may ultimately refine our differentiation of the disorders of personality—whether or not the borderline concept is retained or abandoned—there exists clearly a large group of patients whose intense rage and despair can bring about various retaliatory and aversive responses in psychiatric residents and other beginning therapists. John T. Maltsberger and Dan H. Buie discuss in their chapter the way in which the raw neediness, hatred, and other primitive emotions in such patients can evoke disturbing anxiety and other impulses in the therapist, who may act them out destructively toward the patient unless he is helped to understand and master them.

Maltsberger and Buie stress the particular importance of the role of supervision, and of the supervisor's relationship with the therapist, in treating these difficult patients. An open, trusting collaboration between the trainee and the supervisor can help to sustain the therapeutic process. It will facilitate the detection of avoidance or other potentially dangerous responses on the therapist's part. With the recognition and working through of his own hostile and other negative responses the therapist will be able to develop empathy with his patient and the treatment can proceed more usefully.

Early in this century Adolf Meyer was teaching his students how life experience shaped personality. Since the 1940s the tendency in American psychiatry has been more and more not only to understand how experience is a factor in development, but also to employ psychological intervention as a treatment device intended to modify the patient's patterns of adaptation. Psychoanalysis was an important influence in bringing about this development. The supervision of such psychotherapeutic efforts has become a central part of training in most programs of general psychiatry.

The method of supervision in psychotherapy initially was much influenced by that evolved in the American psychoanalytic institutes. Psychoanalytic educators in the 1920s and 1930s were very concerned with the supervision of the work of student psychoanalysts. By the time the psychoanalytic influence became so marked in American psychiatric residency training, the psychoanalytic institutes had evolved a tripartite teaching program based on (1) personal psychoanalysis (training analysis), (2) individual supervision of several cases in analysis with the candidate (control analyses), and (3) a series of seminars. Classical psychoanalysis as taught in most of the institutes is a treatment designed for neurotic cases, and the supervision practiced in psychoanalytic education has been evolved from experiences with neurotic patients. It is also important to bear in mind that the usual psychoanalytic candidate has had considerable experience in general psychiatry before beginning his control analyses and has resources for personal support and assistance, including the training analysis, that are usually not available to the beginner in psychiatric learning.

The usual practice of the supervising psychoanalyst is to leave the subjective experience of his trainee to the training analysis; as such, it is not considered appropriate for supervision. However correct this educational plan may be for teaching classical psychoanalysis, we believe a modification is necessary in teaching psychotherapy of borderlines to novices. As he begins psychiatric residency the young physician must cope with sudden changes in his therapeutic role and environment and with feeling the acute humiliation that he is so ignorant. Medical school and often an internship have accustomed him to objectify patients to a considerable extent. "Treating the patient as a whole person" in practice most often means taking a brief social history, discouraging too much communication of conflict or emotion-laden material, and treatment through action (a medicine, advice, or physical intervention with instruments may be prescribed). This kind of selective listening and responding with active prescription takes place in the general hospital in which the physician is "captain;" there he issues orders, expects to have them followed, is the most knowledgeable about illness, and takes primary responsibility for treatment.

When the young physician begins his training in psychotherapy, he must accustom himself to a way of proceeding quite different from that to which he has been previously schooled. He must learn to encourage, instead of discourage, discussion of emotion-laden conflicts and relationships and to discourage too much discussion of body complaints. Even more difficult to learn for most is the lesson that inaction in the therapist is the best medicine much of the time. He is no longer able to have his orders followed by nurses and others without question, and he must accustom himself to working as a part of a treatment "team." The process of changing role and environment involves many elements of loss, and first-year trainees in psychiatry are in a state of narcissistic shock as they make the required adaptations.

The fresh resident differs from a psychoanalytic candidate in level of experience, in knowledge, in solidity of professional identification, and in the support resources available. These differences alone make necessary some modification of the standard supervisory process based on the psychoanalytic model. It is also the case that responsibility for care and treatment of a large number of borderline and psychotic patients is placed in the hands of the psychiatric novice. Since these patients differ from psychoanalytic patients in the quality and impact of the transference and in their readiness to act out destructively, they call for different therapy techniques. These different techniques demand further modifications in the methods of supervision.

In this chapter we are especially concerned with problems posed in supervising residents in work with borderline patients. The literature on psychiatric supervision abounds with references to the stressful first psychiatric training year.[4,6,7,15] We have already referred to several of the stresses involved, but in our opinion the greatest stress by far is the instinctual, affective stimulation the resident must endure as he is regularly closeted with borderline and psychotic patients. The imperative and intense quality of the transference that borderline cases evince may set up a flood of reactive feeling in the apprentice therapist that threatens to swamp him. Countertransference reactions involving counteraffects of motherly caring, malice, and aversion will always be called forth. These reactions must be attended to in the supervisory work if a therapeutic relationship is to be achieved and maintained and if the therapist's professional growth is to be ensured.

Daniel Schuster and his colleagues[14] have provided an extensive and useful critical review of the literature on psychiatric supervision. In a helpful way they describe the variety and divergence of opinion on this subject. The literature embraces some views that contradict our philosophy of teaching; certain authors always tend to leave the subjective experience of the apprentice therapist alone and to avoid any "psychotherapeutic" intervention with him, concentrating only on work with material presented by the patient, his problems, and his needs.[16] Other authors, with views similar to ours, believe exploration of the personal responses of the trainee is an essential part of the teaching and learning experience.[4,5,8,15]

It is probable that the reluctance of many supervisors to deal with the trainee's subjective experience partly results from a continued application of a relatively unmodified model of psychoanalytic supervision to the training of residents in general psychiatry. A teaching approach that avoids countertransference review may fit reasonably well in psychiatric training when the patient in treatment is neurotic, but it is not appropriate when the supervisor is trying to help a beginner in his work with a borderline patient.

The inexperience of residents, their lack of knowledge of the quality of life as the borderlines live it, and the intensely stressful affects evoked in working with borderlines are the considerations that make it important to include subjective, countertransference responses in the supervision of work with these patients.

THE PECULIAR STRESSFULNESS OF BORDERLINE PATIENTS

Borderline people typically are harrowed by a sense of aloneness, and in their relations with others are tortured by alternating horrors of abandonment and engulfment. In order to relieve their exhausting inner despair, these patients exhibit a strong tendency to act impulsively and to defend with denial, projection, and splitting. Otto F. Kernberg and Gerald Adler have described these patients, who are to be found in every acute psychiatric ward.[1,2,9,10,11]

A withdrawn, hallucinating schizophrenic patient has abandoned relationships to other people to a considerable degree and is primarily related to his own mental images and inventions, although some relatedness to the real world is maintained. Such a person makes only a tentative relationship with a therapist and is ever ready to retreat to his private inner life that is populated by creatures of his own making. At the opposite extreme lies the neurotic patient, whose basic capacity for relatedness to others is not in question. Such a person will maintain his ties to others through affliction and hardship. Neurotic patients may fantasy about suicide, but it is a most unusual neurotic who is capable of translating the thought into action.

Between the schizophrenic's highly tentative relatedness to others and the neurotic's durable attachment stands the borderline patient in a suicidal crisis. Before the decision is made to kill himself, the borderline patient maintains ties to other people, including the psychotherapist, but the relationships are very painful and express the patient's fundamental mistrust as to the reliability and constancy of others. The affects experienced and expressed by the patient are likely to be extremely intense—much more intense than those of the usual neurotic—and often will have a special quality of eeriness, desperation, and hate. The peculiar intensity and quality of feelings that borderline patients experience evoke intense reactions in others, often the reaction of helpless fear. When a first-year resident is already feeling helpless because of his role change, the countertransference burden of helpless fear that a borderline evokes may be very difficult to bear.

The countertransference distress that a borderline patient arouses is greatly heightened by the preparedness of the patient to do to his therapist and to all others that which he has so much feared would be done to himself. Suicide can be seen as an act of abandoning all others. To the extent that the therapist has abandonment fears of his own, the threat of suicide from his patient is apt to heighten his anxiety and to make him hate the patient.

The capacity of borderline patients to weigh, decide upon, and carry out a suicidal act not only burdens the psychotherapist with helplessness and abandonment dreads, but further taxes him because in reality the patient's life may be at stake. In the treatment of neurotic patients errors arising from destructive countertransference trends, while unfortunate, are usually remediable. Countertransference errors in treating borderline patients at a suicidal crisis have a special extra valence—they may precipitate suicide. The fact that countertransference has a special danger and importance in treating such patients is in itself an additional burden that is likely to produce an aversive response in him who has to shoulder it.

THE EMPATHIC IMPASSE

A highly anxious resident, even if he does not act out by punishing or rejecting, will have difficulty in developing an appropriately empathic relationship with a patient when his instincts cry out for fight or flight. Sadistic countertransference impulses arouse guilt and heighten the expectation that the supervisor will criticize and punish. Tension and withholding result, and this state of affairs often gives rise to a sterile supervisory relationship that parallels an unproductive therapeutic relationship. The resident, afraid of his supervisor and unable to obtain necessary support and assistance with his personal distress, is unable to develop the necessary rapport with his overwhelmed patient. If actual withdrawal does not take place, empathic withdrawal is very likely to occur, and this can only be understood as an aversive countertransference act. Such an act is frequently turned to the service of keeping sadistic impulses out of mind.

That psychotherapy cannot proceed without empathy is evident, and sometimes, especially when aversion in the therapist is marked, the patient may be lost through suicide. But the implications of this kind of empathic impasse go farther. A nihilistic attitude toward the psychotherapeutic treatment of such patients may develop and lead toward constriction of professional development. While it is not necessary to point out that many skilled therapists choose not to treat such patients for reasons that have nothing to do with a failure to develop the necessary empathic capacity, it is nevertheless true that others avoid such cases because in the course of training exactly such a failure took place. We believe that this must often be the consequence of insufficient supervisory support and neglect of the need for education in the matter of countertransference.

NEED FOR SUSTAINING AND SUPPORT FROM SUPERVISORS

Beyond the limitation of professional growth is the matter of symptom development in the trainee. The fact that a high proportion of psychiatrists in training seek out psychotherapy and psychoanalysis is not only because personal treatment experience is wanted for professional training; neither is it because residents are a particularly disturbed group of people. They are men and women under stress who may be compared to combat troops, required by duty to endure great strain without surrendering ground. Anxiety and depression are always frequent in such circumstances, and the supervisor can do much to render the experience less painful and more profitable if he is prepared to lend assistance, support, and understanding, particularly in the area of the resident's emotional response to his disturbing patients.[8]

Supervision in psychotherapy with any kind of patient is an effort to assist in the development of mature and realistic treatment attitudes, the capacity for empathic understanding, and the acquisition of technical skills and professional knowledge. The development of therapeutic maturity and the capacity for empathy are not matters of intellectual learning alone; they involve emotional learning and identification with the supervisor.[3]

The indispensable sustaining and supporting aspects of supervisory technique have been described in the monograph edited by Elvin Semrad and David van Buskirk.[15] Of particular importance when a beginner is working with a borderline patient are the reassuring, bolstering efforts of the supervisor. The supervisor should be prepared to show his trainee how to proceed, to provide him an opportunity to air his feelings, and to reassure him of his competence to learn and to help. The supervisor must also be prepared to share his own experiences in working with such patients, to offer clarifications of the treatment material, and, especially when the trainee tends to deny countertransference, to confront him supportively and constructively.[1]

Correct sustaining and supporting are particularly important in helping with troublesome affects that borderline cases experience and with the uncomfortable reciprocal responses that they arouse.

Countertransference responses to neurotic patients are easier for the usual psychiatric apprentice to bear because the affects are usually without eerie or uncanny quality, but subjective response to borderline cases may involve just such affects, evoked by the primitive emotions of patients who struggle with a sense of utter aloneness and abandonment. In addition, borderline patients exhibit quantitatively great amounts of the more familiar affects of fear, despair, and rage. Because these affects are all experienced by the patient in the mode of an infant, the mouth and teeth are usually the seats of transference impulses, directed at the skin, especially the torso and genitalia, of the apprentice.

According to the needs of the student, the supervisor will offer appropriate sustaining and supporting, including the sharing of his own subjective experience, in order to increase the student's capacity to withstand, and then understand, his own affective responses to the patient. By referring back and forth to the patient's material and to the countertransference experience, the apprentice can see how intimately related the two phenomena may be. He can discern the close connection between his countertransference responses and the patient's life experience, with increasing empathic capacity and understanding.

LEARNING ABOUT BORDERLINE LIFE EXPERIENCE

The usual resident is comparatively unfamiliar with certain primitive affect states and needs to be taught about them in supervision, if possible, *before* they come to play an important part in the patient's material as the treatment develops. From the very beginning, the supervisor needs to direct the resident's attention to the patient's affect.

Useful illustrative material from literature, painting, and motion pictures may be brought in. For example, Joyce Carol Oates's novel, *Wonderland,* suggests something of the experience of gruesome aloneness at the hands of an uncaring and murderous parent. Franz Kafka's fiction, the work of the Norwegian artist Edvard Munch, and the film *2001* are all evocative of a sense of devastating, sometimes ghastly, solitude.

Concentration on the affective experience of the patient and an effort to imagine for oneself what the patient feels lead naturally into a discussion of what feelings the patient evokes in the therapist and his supervisor.

Residents employ a variety of defenses in order to keep out of mind the distressing impulses and affects stirred up by, and complementary to, the impulses and affects of their patients. Hate presents the major problem, and supervisors must be alert to the particular defenses that a trainee at any one time may be using. It is important not only to assist the resident by helping him observe his countertransference but also to help him avert destructive action that is certain to ensue if the countertransference remains out of awareness.[13]

Projection of destructive impulses onto the patient may lead to inappropriate anxiety about suicidal danger or to ill-grounded fears of homicidal outbreak not objectively evident in the interview material. The apprentice therapist may feel inappropriately discouraged or inadequate to the therapeutic task if his countertransference anger is turned on himself. Excessive solicitude for the patient's welfare is sometimes a signal that a reaction formation against the countertransference is taking place, and isolation against the hatred is often indicated by a bland indifference to interview material that would be blood-chilling under ordinary circumstances. Denial of suicidal danger may indicate considerable unconscious rage against the patient.

DEVELOPING THE CAPACITY TO TOLERATE AND USE COUNTERTRANSFERENCE FEELINGS

To the extent that the supervisor is experienced as trustworthy, helpful, and knowledgeable, he will be an object of emulation and thus can lend himself to the formation of the apprentice's professional skill and ego ideal. One of the requirements of a mature therapist is the capacity to tolerate a wide range of affects and impulses in himself, to bear them consciously without guilt, and to restrain himself from acting on them. The range includes both sexual and destructive impulses, but the average psychiatrist in training is likely to have difficulty in acknowledging, bearing, and getting into perspective his malicious reactions to patients. The more intense the sadistic excitation becomes, the more superego anxiety rises. The tendency is to act out aversively and avoid relationship to the patient. It is useful to think of malice and aversion as reciprocally coordinated elements in countertransference hate, the latter being proportional to the intensity of the former.

The ego capacity to bear a variety of impulses is usually one that must be gradually developed during the years of residency training. It is often facilitated by personal analysis, in which the superego is modified, and yields the necessary territory to the ego so that patient-related impulses and instincts no longer give rise to guilt and anxiety. While we believe that personal psychoanalysis is ultimately necessary for anyone who wishes to work psychotherapeutically with borderline patients, the supervisory relationship can also contribute to increasing self-tolerance as the apprentice is offered the opportunity to identify with a supervisor who is comfortable with his own countertransference affects, including the bloodthirsty and torturing impulses that most borderline patients provoke.

Having initiated a discussion of the affects experienced by the borderline patient, the supervisor may notice evidence, as psychotherapy proceeds, of superego anxiety. The trainee may tend to withhold material, to behave in a self-protective manner, or otherwise to indicate a sense of guilt. The supervisor may be in a position to infer empathically what it is that his student finds difficult to bear and to lend the necessary assistance, possibly by sharing some of his own subjective experience evoked by similar patients under similar circumstances.

HAZARDS OF ATTACHMENT BETWEEN THE PATIENT AND THERAPIST

The phase of transference hatred that is so likely to stir up reciprocal destructive impulses in the therapist is typically preceded by a period of transference idealization and longing. The idealization appeals to residuals of the infantile narcissism of the beginner therapist, intensifies his longing to rescue the patient from the grips of illness, and heightens his omnipotent self-expectations to perform the therapeutic tour de force that the patient so confidently expects from him. The magical expectations of the patient excite the magical expectations of the tyro. It will not be apparent to either that these expectations are for perpetual holding and nurturance. When the patient is inevitably disappointed, the loving expectations give way to transference hate. The therapist, in turn, is likely to be flooded with anxiety over the loss of his own hopes of infantile togetherness and omnipotence. Inevitably countertransference impulses of malice and aversion arise; they are difficult to tolerate consciously and are likely to be managed with the defenses previously outlined, ones that allow them to be acted out unless assistance is forthcoming from the supervisor.

If correctly supervised, the resident can be prepared for this frequent kind of crisis. He comes to recognize the transference–countertransference loving togetherness that is the inevitable prelude to disappointment and to transference–countertransference hate. As he develops an appropriate sensitivity to early steps in this scenario, the resident comes to appreciate these steps as the signals of danger to the therapeutic alliance.

THE SUPERVISORY ALLIANCE

It should be borne in mind that the supervisory review of the resident's subjective experience with his borderline patient has as its aims (1) the development of the capacity to bear a variety of impulses in consciousness without anxiety, (2) the promotion of empathic capacity, and (3) the prophylaxis against regressive acting out of countertransference impulses in the therapeutic relationship. None of these aims is likely to be attained unless the supervisor is able to not only provide but also protect a relationship of trust and collaboration with his trainee. Considerable sensitivity is required, and the countertransference review cannot be conducted in an intrusive way. The supervisor must maintain an attitude of helpful neutrality toward the countertransference material volunteered by the apprentice who, after all, is called upon to surrender considerable privacy if he is to work in this way with his supervisor.

The supervisor must be prepared to sacrifice some of his own privacy and take the lead in reviewing with his trainee the nature of his subjective responses to the patient's material. This requires, of course, that the supervisor should be sufficiently comfortable with his own responses so that he is not made anxious by the possible responses of his apprentice.

From time to time it may happen that the trainee will tend to devaluate the supervisor, denying his own impulses and projecting them onto the teacher. This is usually the consequence of exposing too much too fast. It can be compared in effect to excessively deep interpretation in therapy. While such projection must be watched for and dealt with appropriately, it can also be taken as a signal that the supervisor is not being sufficiently respectful of the trainee's developing, but not yet mature, capacity to bear in consciousness his id derivatives. Correct pacing is essential. This kind of supervision must never be carried out intrusively. Residents may from time to time invite the supervisor to discuss the personal genetic origins of countertransference response. We have not found it necessary to do so and prefer to leave such explorations to personal analysis.

The empathic capacity of an apprentice psychiatrist can be increased, a potentially frightening and sterile patient encounter can be turned into a useful educational experience, and the patient's opportunity to grow can be improved when the supervisor is willing and able to share his own subjective experience in a nonintrusive, sustaining, and supporting manner, while he studies with his trainee the relationship between subjective responses, the patient's transference, and the patient's life history.

REFERENCES

1. Adler G: Valuing and devaluing in the psychotherapeutic process. Arch Gen Psychiatry, 22:454-461, 1960
2. Adler G: Helplessness in the helpers. Br J Med Psychol 45:315-326, 1972
3. Buie DH, Maltsberger JT: Growth and apprenticeship learning, in Semrad EV, van Buskirk D (eds): Teaching Psychotherapy of Psychotic Patients. New York, Grune & Stratton, 1969, pp 92-105
4. Ekstein P, Wallerstein RS: The Teaching and Learning of Psychotherapy. New York, Basic Books, 1963
5. Fleming J, Benedek T: Psychoanalytic Supervision. New York, Grune & Stratton, 1966
6. Halleck SL, Woods SM: Emotional problems of psychiatric residents. Psychiatry 25:339-346, 1962
7. Kahana RJ: Psychotherapy: Models of the essential skill, in Bibring GL (ed): The Teaching of Dynamic Psychiatry. A Reappraisal of the Goals and Techniques in the Teaching of Psychoanalytic Psychiatry. New York, International Universities Press, 1968
8. Kaplowitz D: Teaching empathic responsiveness in the supervisory process of psychotherapy. Am J Psychother 21:774-781, 1967
9. Kernberg OF: Structural derivatives of object relationships. Int J Psychoanal 47:236-253, 1966
10. Kernberg OF: Borderline personality organization. J Am Psychoanal Assoc 15:641-685, 1967

11. Kernberg OF: Treatment of borderline patients, in Giovacchini PL (ed): Tactics and Techniques in Psychoanalytic Therapy. New York, Science House, 1972, pp 254–290

12. Maltsberger JT, Buie DH: The work of supervision, in Semrad EV, van Buskirk D (eds): Teaching Psychotherapy of Psychotic Patients. New York, Grune & Stratton, 1969, pp 65–91

13. Maltsberger J, Buie D: Countertransference hate in the treatment of suicidal patients. Arch Gen Psychiatry 30:625–633, 1974

14. Schuster DB, Sandt JJ, Thaler OF: Clinical Supervision of the Psychiatric Resident. New York, Brunner/Mazel, 1972

15. Semrad E, van Buskirk D (eds): Teaching Psychotherapy of Psychotic Patients. New York, Grune & Stratton, 1969

16. Tarachow S: An Introduction to Psychotherapy. New York, International Universities Press, 1963

Afterword

The diagnoses of borderline personality, borderline states, or just "borderline" have become popular in clinical psychiatry in recent years, especially in the United States. Essays are included in this volume both by clinicians who espouse such terms and find them useful and by other investigators who deplore them as lacking specificity and clarity. Whether the current popularity of the borderline concept is a vogue or a more lasting development will depend upon its ability to generate useful research and further clinical understanding.

The present widespread use of the term "borderline" in this country is a product of the particular history of American psychiatry. Psychoanalytic concepts have found widespread, though far from universal, acceptance here. They have enabled psychiatrists working in hospitals, clinics, and private offices to find meaning in their patients' words and behavior and to offer treatment approaches based on empathic understanding that the coldly descriptive European psychiatry of Emil Kraepelin and his followers seemed to rule out. But in their focus upon underlying meanings and explanatory mechanisms, psychoanalysts sometimes have devoted less attention to the phenomena of psychiatry and the careful description of its disorders.

In the case of the personality or character disorders, whose recognition as identifiable clinical conditions occurred quite late in psychiatry, psychoanalytic developmental and structural concepts and theories of object relationships seemed to offer particular promise. Individuals with personality disorders have lives that are in disorder; they demonstrate multiple problems of ego functioning; and they experience particular difficulty sustaining relationships with other people. It is in this broad group that the borderline syndrome or states seem to belong.

The personality disorders tend to be diagnosed according to the predominant behavioral patterns or personality traits that the patients demonstrate, such as in the case of addictive states, sexual deviations, or antisocial characters. If so, what are we dealing with in the case of the

borderline states? There is no predominant behavioral or characterological pattern that has been consistently described. Indeed, as
Samuel B. Guze points out, the borderline diagnosis does not fulfill the
criteria of any distinct clinical disorder. The borderline state seems, as
Robert P. Knight noted slightly facetiously a "panneurotic character
disorder" (in *Psychoanalytic Psychiatry and Psychology,* vol. 1, International Universities Press, 1954). Indeed Otto F. Kernberg and other
authors who use the borderline terms have included on one occasion or
another patients with alcoholism, narcotic addiction, antisocial behavior,
various forms of impulsive and acting-out behavior, sexual deviation—
practically the whole gamut of the 35 to 40 forms of personality disorder
listed in the DSM-II.* One might think of the borderline as a character
disorder without a particular behavioral specialty. It is true that many
patients who are clearly drug addicts, sexual deviants, or even criminals
are diagnosed as borderline personalities, but often such individuals fail
to rely on any one maladaptive behavioral pattern with sufficient regu-
larity to warrant a more specific diagnosis.

Psychoanalytic structural and developmental concepts help us
understand personality formation and many other clinical phenomena
observed in adult patients. The primitive defense mechanisms observed
by Kernberg in his patients and the tendency of adolescents described by
John Zinner, Edward R. Shapiro, and James F. Masterson to project
elements of their own self-concepts onto their parents or therapists, are
made more intelligible when related to what is known of the early childhood processes of identification and personality formation. I would
argue, however, with the contention that mechanisms such as splitting
and primitive idealization have been shown to be associated regularly and
conclusively with a well-delineated clinical disorder—the borderline—
and not to other psychiatric conditions. Indeed, it appears to me that a
number of the concepts of early object relationships that have been
described in connection with borderline patients are formulated at such a
high level of abstraction that it would be difficult to relate them clearly to
any sharply focused or accurately described clinical condition.

In my opinion the emergence of the borderline diagnosis has led to
fresh understanding of the psychological mechanisms underlying
character pathology. But a price has also been paid. The borderline diagnosis seems often to be used indiscriminately as a catch-all for immature

*The DSM-II (*Diagnostic and Statistical Manual of Mental Disorders,* 2d ed,
American Psychiatric Association, 1968) defines personality disorders as being
characterized by "deeply ingrained maladaptive patterns of behavior that are perceptibly
different in quality from psychotic and neurotic symptoms."

individuals or for patients prone to act in ways that are troublesome to themselves or to others. Sufficient attention has not been paid to the specific behavioral or characterological mechanisms being manifested, and diagnostic understanding has been sacrificed. Psychiatric trainees, for example, seem at times to short circuit their diagnostic thinking by grouping a great variety of personality disorders under the rubric of "borderline."

The personality disorders constitute a broad frontier in psychiatry and psychoanalysis, whose implications we are only beginning to apprehend. Within this large group are perhaps half or more of all the patients seen in clinical practice. There are many types of personality seen both in and out of clinical work—both normal and disturbed individuals—that have yet to be described clearly, let alone understood. In order to understand the riches and strengths as well as the weaknesses and vulnerabilities of personality, much work needs to be done. Many mental mechanisms and phenomena of development at lesser levels of abstraction than those set forth in recent psychoanalytic theoretical discussions remain to be delineated in the psychology of personality types. It is as if several steps in the clarification of the clinical psychology of personality have been bypassed as deeper more "fundamental" explanatory formulations have been sought.

The joining that occurred in the 1920s (through the work of Wilhelm Reich, Franz Alexander, August Aichhorn, and others) of the dynamic approaches of psychoanalysis and the phenomenological orientation of general psychiatry brought significant initial advances in the understanding of neurotic, impulsive, and other character types. A revival in the collaboration of these two orientations is needed for significant progress in the area of the personality disorders to occur. Psychiatrists, who concern themselves with describing and understanding the character disorders, tend to address themselves more to behavior and action and to the alloplastic forms of adaptation and maladaptation at a manifest level. Psychoanalysts and psychoanalytically oriented psychiatrists, on the other hand, pay relatively more attention to affects and personality structure, to the autoplastic functions of character disorder. A blend of both approaches is much needed for clarification in this area.

There is another reason why clear thinking in the field of the character and behavior disorders is of especial importance. This is a major frontier of our field, but it is the one that requires the greatest collaboration with other disciplines. The clinical picture of the personality disorders, more so than in the case of the neuroses and psychoses, is a function of the social context in which the individual is being seen. A static analysis of the structure of personality is not sufficient, for individuals with personality disorders are constantly engaged in various forms of interaction with the environment. They live at the interface of the self and society. They can only be fully understood through a systems point of view that takes into account not only the intrapsychic patterns but also considers the familial, social, and community context. The detection of personality pathology tends to occur in direct relation to differences (in race, sex, class, and age, for example) between patient and observer. Before psychiatry can enter into proper collaboration with sociology, anthropology, and law to understand the personality disorders, we need first to put our own clinical house in order.

Index

DATE DUE

OCT 21 1996		
MAY 7 2000		
DEC 8 2002		
NOV 2003		
JAN 2004		